TO GWEN WITH LOVE

The book, *To Gwen With Love,* is a gesture of affection and respect which is probably unique in the annals of publishing. In a burst of appreciation for the extraordinary woman named Gwendolyn Brooks, members of the Black Chicago community decided during the summer of 1969 to "present roses to the living." The "roses" were to take the shape of a major public "tribute" to be staged in the Black community's principal theater toward the end of the year. The date of December 28 was chosen, and the word went out to Black artists and writers across the country, inviting them to converge on the Affro-Arts Theater for the occasion. And they came—writers, musicians, painters, photographers, actors, dancers—from everywhere for the love-fest. And many who could not be present nevertheless sent their greetings, mostly in the form of poetry. Indeed, for the special tribute to the warm, gentle honoree, who also happens to be one of the world's finest poets, some writers and artists braved the Muse and created their first poems.

The initial idea of the tribute had been the Kuumba Workshop's, a group of Chicago artists who are personally acquainted with the prize-winning poet. The local admirers of Gwendolyn Brooks knew, even if those in other cities did not, of the unselfish dedication of Gwendolyn Brooks, first as woman, then, as mother, as artist and as community worker. While she was acclaimed by the world as the first Black winner of a Pulitzer Prize (for *Annie Allen,* a collection of poems, in 1950) and as official poet laureate of the state of Illinois, the Chicagoans responded to her first as the generous resident artist whose home served as "workshop" for aspiring writers and who routinely gave of her time and funds to encourage literary talent wherever she found it. Artists in other cities either had been touched by her quiet magic in person or else knew her by reputation, but it is fair to assume that none paid her homage merely on the basis of her great public fame.

The tribute to Gwendolyn Brooks was an overwhelming success, and when it was over, the idea of permanently memorializing the event in a book seemed to follow naturally. Led by Val Gray Ward and Patricia L. Brown, a community delegation presented the publishing idea to John H. Johnson, who added the project to his Book Division list. That is how—and why—*To Gwen With Love* became a reality.

H.W.F.

TO GWEN WITH LOVE
*An Anthology dedicated to
Gwendolyn Brooks*

Edited by
Patricia L. Brown
Don L. Lee
and Francis Ward

Johnson Publishing Company, Inc.
Chicago: 1971

Acknowledgments

Thanks are due to the following for permission to include previously published selections.

Broadside Press, for "Gwendolyn Brooks," copyright © 1969 by don l. lee from *Don't Cry, Scream;* and for "The Sun Came" and "To Gwendolyn Brooks," copyright © 1968 by Etheridge Knight from *Poems from Prison.*

Negro Digest, for "A Live Celebration" by Sarah Webster Fabio from September/October *Negro Digest;* and for "For Eusi, Ahi Kewi and Gwen Brooks" from June 1969 *Negro Digest.* Used by permission of the authors.

South and West, for "His Body is an Eloquence" by Pinkie Gordon Lane, from *South and West,* vol. 8, nos. 2-3, copyright © by Sue Abbott Boyd.

Library of Congress Catalog No. 76-128456

SBN Nos. 87485-043-6 (cloth), 87485-044-4 (paper)

Printed in the United States of America

Editors' Note

Kuumba—that's creativity, the creativity that cleanses, purifies, creates the consciousness of a people/nation. Kuumba—that's a group of black artists in Chicago, founded by Val Gray Ward—dancers, players, artists, musicians, singers, writers, black artists/people who welcomed the idea of celebrating Gwendolyn Brooks.

From Kuumba came this book, came a celebration on December 28, 1969 at the Affro-Arts Theater in Chicago that said "we luv you Sister Gwendolyn." That luv is shared by the black people to/for/from whom this black woman/poet writes.

Hers is the poetry that cleanses, purifies, makes whole and creates the consciousness of a people.

We are grateful. Hence this anthology.

Sister Gwendolyn bees a Kuumba player, too.

P.L.B., D.L.L., F.W.

January, 1970

Note: Proceeds from the sale of this anthology will be used to support the Gwendolyn Brooks Library housed in the Black Women's Committee House in Chicago, Illinois. This black education/culture/community center is run by the Black Woman's Committee for the Protection and Care of Our Children.

Contents

For the blak people to/for/from
whom Gwendolyn Brooks writes and for
Gwen, with our love, BLAKLUV

Introduction

This is a book of poems to a poet.

It is a collective gesture by leading black poets in honor of the presence and witness of Gwendolyn Brooks, who is also a poet and a poem.

Out of a sense of indebtedness and responsibility, the poets in this volume composed special poems of thanks to the Pulitzer Prize winner and the Poet Laureate of Illinois. And thus we have a book which is an extraordinary gesture of love and perhaps the most unprecedented act of communal generosity in the cultural history of Afro-Americans.

Never before has there been a gesture of this magnitude for a living black poet.

Never before have so many expressed so much appreciation through so many poets of eminence.

One can say, in fact, that this event marks a milestone in the cultural history of Afro-Americans. For a *community* is speaking through these poets. And that community is saying that it is no longer necessary for our seers and sayers to go to strangers for prizes and honors. The community is saying that it is now awarding its own prizes. And, as we all know, there can be no higher award than the approbation and appreciation of people who walked the same road with you, carrying the same wooden beams on their backs.

Some prophets *are* honored in their own time and in their own communities, especialy if they reflect their own time and if they remain in their own communities. Gwendolyn Brooks is an exemplary manifestation of that fact. Though born in Topeka, Kansas, she was reared in Chicago and has lived there, in the heart of the black community, most of her life. She was married in black Chicago to writer Henry Blakely, and her two children, Nora and Henry, were born there. Her poems celebrate the truth of her life. They celebrate the truth of blackness, which is also the truth of man. They reflect the wholeness of a person with deep roots in the soil of her people. It is fashionable in some white literary circles to say that "the sweet and lyrical" Gwendolyn Brooks has been sidetracked by the "demon of militancy." But this attitude is simply a reflection of the enormous ignorance of the white culture structure. For

Gwendolyn Brooks has always been committed and lyrical and relevant. Before it was fashionable, she was tone deep in blackness. In the fifties, she was writing poems about Emmett Till and Little Rock and the black boys and girls who came North looking for the Promised Land and found concrete deserts. In fact, she has always written about the sounds and sights and flavors of the black community. Her poems are distinguished by a bittersweet lyricism and an overwhelming concreteness. They are filled with names like Big Bessie, Mrs. Martin's Booker T., Mae Belle and Pearl May Lee, with images of broken bottles, pool rooms, roses in whiskey glasses, onion fumes and yesterday's garbage, the Club DeLisa and the Rhumboogie, "illegible landlords," rooms full of beads and receipts, and love in "the crowding darkness" of the ghetto at midnight in May. Gwendolyn Brooks was there—she heard the screams, felt the pains, saw the blood, laughed the laughs. And one should give her words, all her words, their full weight.

This tribute grew out of a feeling of awe which a number of black artists feel in the presence of Miss Brooks's testimony. It also grew out of a sense of communal responsibility, out of a sense that the black community must now assume responsibility for the support and recognition of public monuments like Gwendolyn Brooks. Somebody was saying somewhere late one night that Gwen Brooks was beautiful and that the black community should tell her while she is still blooming in our hearts. And Val Gray Ward, who said it first, helped to organize it; and soon, all over America, people were putting down on pieces of paper what they thought about this extraordinary woman, who was telling it like it was before some of us were born. And we knew that all this would embarrass her, for she has never sought the spotlight. But we also knew that there was history to be served and that it was necessary to let the living and the unborn know that we had a proper appreciation for service and sacrifice and elegant and relevant language in defense of mankind. The grand outcome was this volume which spans the generations of black culture. Margaret Walker is represented here and Samuel Allen and Dudley Randall and Margaret Danner and John Killens. There are also contributions from the new generation of poets, from don lee, Etheridge Knight, nikki giovanni, sonia sanchez, Zack Gilbert and Eugene Perkins. In a sense, however, it is inappropriate to speak of the generations of black poets. For this volume indicates that there is no generation gap in black poetry. Particularly noticeable is the appreciation of Miss Brooks expressed by the younger poets.

In different tones and accents and with varying degrees of success, the contributors attempt to capture the poet's spirit, comparing her to a "spirit-light," a ship ("precise and honed"), and an African queen or goddess. In the opinion of the contributors, the poet is "slender, shy, sensitive," with "skin deep velvet night," a voice like bells and "black words of fire and blood."

Let there be no mistake about it: Gwen Brooks is being honored here not only because of the quality of her poetry but also because of the quality of her life. And by all this we mean to say that she *is* a poem. She is a poem of commitment and dedication to her craft and her community, she is a poem which teaches us the value of vision and will and growth, she is a poem which vibrates with our inner dynamics, she is grace in free verse, she is a lesson, she is a sermon, she is a rhyme, a rhythm, a Reality.

Jean-Paul Sartre said once that it is harder to live than to write books. Gwendolyn Brooks said the same thing once in a poem about a woman who made poetry out of *the act* of boiling eggs. "Being you," Gwendolyn Brooks wrote, "you cut your poetry from wood." One could say the same thing about Gwendolyn Brooks. She cuts her poetry from wood and stone and steel.

POETRY

To Gwen Brooks

light, light, LIGHT

natural LIGHT;
i mean naturally SPIRIT*LIGHT.
yellow, and indigo,
violet, and blue,
        hue you.
orange and green,
and orange and LIGHT.
did you, did you seeee thaatt?
aehh, here it comes again
        mmmm-blamm
feel it? feel thatt-
        nature-LIGHT.
hummmmmmmmmmmmmhhhmmmmmmmmmmmmmm
mmaaaahhhhh yea,
        it's
        GWENDOLYN BROOKS***

spiritual cleanliness
pome for gwen. in upper south. chicago

lower south. in bushlike african villages of the afric tribe
in memphis. in scarboro village. where our ancestors sleep
with wide open doors. and flowers are flowers

lower south. upper south

i create to celebrate the
presence of gods and goddesses. feel my soul
and touch the trees of life in my pomes. part of my energies
know. my background is baptist
that. sometimes my soul gets happy. my background is happiness

the day. the time. the schedule. the thot. the aftermath. now
the child. the love. the school. dead
the walk. up chicago. across playgrounds. gravel roads. dirty sidewalks.
puddles of clouded waters. on rainy days. dry days. them days. after
rainy nights.
splash. the movements. the step. the dance.

(sing)
jump back honey jump back. jump back honey jump back

the dip. the duck. the riff. of our quick nigger legs. right on
diddy bopping all up and down battlefields with buster browns. kicking

(sing)
gwen gwen
in the world again
gwen gwen in the world again
gwen gwen we gonna win gwen gwen in the world again

the future is. the past is. the past is. the future. is our future. is

(sing)
love your elders love your elders love your elders and you will live again

o gwen do lyn
o you goddess of all the beautiful sounds. right on
o young warriors and lovers
    in the faces of the old see yourself
    now smile at your beauty

(sing)
gwen gwen   gwen gwen
in the world again   in the world again

(sing)
singing the song of life. singing the song of life
singing the song of life. my life
singing the song of life. my life

this is the new dawn. where are the fruits of our queen's womanhood
how long. how long. for happiness. even ripen fruit turns to earth
i feel. i feel the divine spirits of god with a passionate love ex-
tended beyond the terrestrial heavens of the universe. i pray. i pray
for wisdom of those blinded by centuries of false prophets all up
and down our minds.
nations dying. debating over the american rag. while feeble minded
monsters peep from behind closed locked doors.
niggers. stepping. happily. on their future selves
getting down. in buster browns. praising
four letters words. swearing against almighty gods and goddesses
of our lives. shouting

(sing)
no respect. no respect no respect no respect no respect well
no more lord   no mo   no more lord   no mo   no more lord   no mo

no more women being men. in the new nation. of our minds
beauty is beauty here. so let obscenities fall below. beneath the
soul of our feet. no hiked skirts. showing creaked faces to the
world of any beast dripping semen from sores of hopelessness marks.
the scag. the scag. the scag ain't no warrior's mark

this is the new dawn

seeds are cast into the earth. into a womb
and new things appear
i will love you. i will love you as the honeysuckle vines smell
of happiness. i will love you as i walk the new path to freedom
as i pick flowers along the dusty road to my village hut. i will feel
the images of
natural beauty
in the trees. in the leaves
beneath the skies. of my mind

i am filled with god and all divine thots
i have glimpsed at the future of my life in your face
i will smile forever now
wishing for seasons of old age to ripen me
salaam my natural haired sister. salaam

The Wreath
for Gwendolyn Brooks

Deft
easily above
the ship's gleam
     levels
     in the far place
is honed,
precise,
is power and complete.

The whim
     of the thoroughbred
may, or may not be
the swift race,
but is poised
spare
incomparably fleet.

The sloop, lean
   leans
     into the wind
   slits
     the clean wave
in sheer pursuit
    to gain
if it deign
     the wreath.

for gwendolyn brooks—a whole & beautiful spirit
. . . an act of living is an act of love—David Llorens

in the beginning was the sight
of blackness & was the seed
a sight which lives an act of love
a cite of images/creation of
where we must go & where we must be
(& also why
(listen to her eyes as they see us
a sight of poems blackpoems
peoplepoems poems for directions/finders
site movers moving image values
moving to cite beauty moving to
proclaim love & other holy things
(& sight reflections of poet/being
written & spoken & heard from cite seed
vibrations which are
(for she is a sure direction/voice
(which makes us brittle in ourselves
moving selfhate moving dross
changing moving toward the cite
of blackness beginning from the seed
beginning from her sight which is
an act of love which is an act of
life

*Upon dedication of the Gwendolyn Brooks Library, Black Women's
Committee House, Chicago, Illinois, March 23, 1969*

a voice above the wind

gwendolyn brooks is   trusty is warm as
she reads cozy-voice   likes being sister-
not mattering the caller's age but is
wild splash torrents words in picture
signs pealaway—ticky/tack tofind
            the bodieswhere
indifference playedgodlostman
and never knew-she
            as if angry
            as if plainness
by their standard still
            can think can dream will do
she-gwen-blakely-brooks be dreamer is sharer too

June, 1968

Mama

    Her face is a meditative frown,
her life is a smile for the world. Rough
Life has turned her mouth down. The
frown is the antonym of herself. Her words
are a spotlight that show the world
truth, while her eyes calm or quake
the earth. Cold or warm, her face,
words, and eyes transmit the smile
of life love.

Gwen; words
pretty or precise
won't come now
each dust the other
to work this space. I wait.
I wait
a line
of
simple grace
to
thump down my trumpet
and sing; love
to u love
u be
u be all
u be all th'
u be all th' love
u be all th' love
u be
u do be
u do be
u do be
u do be love love
love do be u
do be u do be u do be u love
love be love in u love
make me love u be love
u be love
u be love
u be love
u be love

A Bird in the City
for Gwendolyn Brooks

They held her up to me.
"See," they said, "your kind can make it."
I wouldn't look.
Too many times I'd seen teeth-smiles,
Carbon faces suited and scrubbed,
Dull eyes weak from the hurt,
I wouldn't look.
Then, my head lightened
As they read her songs. I
Felt a smile, it was warm,
Faces were scrubbed and clean,
And I looked.
Her eyes knew the hurt
Yet called for hope, I stood, exalted,
A bird in the city was singing.

To Gwen Brooks

1
we
    never saw her
we-meaning
me-
    and
        the other cats
that dug poetry
once
    or twice
        we saw
pictures
          of some
gentle
        black lady-smiling
knowingly-
           knowingly like
             she knew
we were looking

2
you
    ever see
a black lady
        smile?
huh?
    a black lady
smile-
        teeth shining
eyes
pouring
        forth wisdom
you

ever see
a black lady
            smile beauty?

3
this
            dude ralph
dug her 'we
                    real cool'
and ralph-
                    ralph read
the hell
            out of it
when
            he finished
we was cool/
                    like that

4
(her poem/standing on a wet page)
last
            night i touched
a page
                    it felt
like any
                    other
piece of paper
                    cool coarse
nothing exceptionally
                    moving-you know
and i couldn't
                    figure out why
my eyes

                    were wet
until i remembered
                    the words/

5
and
      now poets
reach
          deep for
new words
      to describe her
new pictures
                    to project
with sweeping
                    hands
                          reaching
deep
      to turn
              words
into caresses
            and
                  caresses
into
      heart
she has
          touched ours
and it
          is with
deep
      appreciation
                    that we
touch
          hers/

Black Children
This is the urgency: Live
            And have your blooming in the noise of the whirlwind.
                                            —Gwendolyn Brooks

Like hungry birds
searching a winter land
for bread tossed on snow,
are black children.

Spring buds caught
in the swirl
                of wet leaves,
                            falling away from their tree.

But in Chicago, a poetess sings the second sermon
and with her poems conceives their life.

Francois Clemmons

Dedicated to the living memory of Miss Gwendolyn Brooks

1

O heavy black woman of mother-confidence and life-weight
You arose at dawn and died at dusk
Leaving me the echoes of unironed shirts and torn underwear.
I can't buy you new shoes for your tired feet,
The brown rocker with its sagging pillows
Won't soothe your aching back,
And your night-bed won't rock you across Jordan.
Come to me sweet Mother of Life.
I have an earthly balm and a promise of no miracles.
Leave your pain and self pity at the river side,
Jesus can get them when he comes to call.

2

My Aunt Hattie,
        who belonged to the generation that composed spirituals,
Always blessed the table before dinner.
She surely knew He answered her prayer before she even began
(It was only for us to wait and see).
Aunt Hattie was real light and had blue eyes.
She knew Ol' Mastuh, the Devil's own,
Raped her mama in the field one day,
But no man had ever touched her.

Praise Due
      to Gwen Brooks!

Success
does not seem
to have spoiled
Gwen Brooks.
There she was
riding on the El—
I tapped her
on the shoulder
"Are you Miss Brooks?"
I whispered.
"Yes," she smiled warmly.
And my heart
sang later
as tears fell
from my eyes.
Gwen Brooks is Human
Gwen Brooks Lives Love
Gwen Brooks Still Smiles
Gwen Brooks Has Time for
Black People
Gwen Brooks reads Black Writers' Writing
Gwen Brooks evokes tears of joy
at her humanness.
GWEN BROOKS
      IS.

Fishing
After Gwen & other precious stones: the black quartet

1. **brooks and stones**

I
walk self-conscious
without a sky
or even
an alternative shadow
of a tree.

I
found no castle
in your care
nor ermine underneath
your wool.
Nor a woman
behind the girlish face.
Just another female
with detachable charms.

But there was a thirst
if not delight
to put a limit to the roof/

But of sadness
there was size and weight
and pity
for the sight
of pleasures mating with the wolves.

You lie
with fixed eyes water-filled
swaying

with a single touch.

We lay
dreaming of the flood
that brings no real conclusion
to the gloom.
We lie
one to the other
as we fish.

2. **rippling shadows**

I
am doomed
like hercules.

What does it matter?

if stretched out
on a barbed wire bed
or the unyielding tip
upon each breast
filled with the hollow moistures of the night
the greenness of the moon
as you rush away
an unapproachable fury
hissing
with pale gaunt dragon pets
you dip in blackness
drained from thunder tea.

if bewitched

into a rose
trellised
on the lean
and deadly riddles
your
static
smile
creates

how to blossom
in the unfamiliar air

how to embrace
the reckless
size
of
you?

3. **river voices**

Why do you hide?

and press your face
where even the sun must blink
in the light
that blackness brings
as you press your thoughts
where thunder
hums mahalia's chant
and keeps the secret
of your grove
that blossoms

in
sheer
space.

You are
fastidious.

choosing
to sway
in a phantom breeze
allowing no more
than a crescent shadow of your self
to
filter
to
my
feet.

You are fastidious
will probably haunt
some other ground with grieving
when
I
am
dead.

Your choice:

tomorrow's orchids
pruned today
like lena's hair
and billie's hands
and nina's closing eyes.

sarah's melting flawless riff
and ella's gleam
or dinah's voice
still smothered in the ashes
that were flesh
or drowned
in lightning's heavy milk.

fastidious
and fine
and long ago
where only shadows
dream and sport
above the staff
not even dragon wings can reach
softer than space
or voices of the long deceased.

4. **brown earth & lace: a riff**

graded
to
vital
gleaming
brown
fashioned
to the cult
of personal shape
where
elliptical
seamless lines
breed
more feeling

than balboa's lace

stretching
from an Aztec temple
to a star

that broods
upon
the
moon

where
sleep
comes crashing through
to fullness
and other colors
close to
black

to the edge
where
quiet
drifts.

As Critic
Second of the Gwendolyn Brooks sequence

Gwendolyn Brooks
  was usually as quiet
    as the flow of water that her name evokes,

      yet she would more than murmur
        when encountering
          a less than smooth bedrock of verse.

        She would wash the slime
          of inversions (leechy clingers)
            and cliches that barnacle flowing verse,
              away.

          She would be a refreshing sip
            to caterpillar-like words,
              especially Black-bogged ones,

            so that after leaving her
              they would more easily trip
                into sun-seeking flutterbys.

R.M. Dennis

To Gwendolyn Brooks

Proud Bearer
of Mother Africa,
bring your gift of blackness
to revolutionize black minds.

Let each verse
strip away our masks
and plant the seed toward nationhood—
the black nationhood
bathed in the heritage
that Malcolm rapped to us about.

You, our priestess
delving into our consciousness with your black-rays
and laying it out before our eyes
to gaze at, to study, then to know
that the now has arrived.
We will heed your words:
"This is the urgency: Live!
And have your blooming in the noise of the whirlwind."

Black Lady's Inspiration

Your head is held high with eyes that
      sparkle like diamonds on a
            sunny day;
Your mind is sound which simplifies
      your actions from
            day to day;
You speak as a black lady with love,
      understanding and
            sincerity;
Your presence is something which I nor
      any man could refuse to
            enjoy;
But yet you're as humble as a lamb asleep
      on a cold winter's
            night;
Your willingness to help would surprise
      many a man and help him on
            his way;
Black Lady, you're the one who keeps a
      Black man, like me
            on my feet
               every day.

To Gwen, with Love

Once
"the poets"
floated in abstractions
called ART
squishing
to respectability
on too much tea
in private
drawing rooms
but you,
Our Sister,
shout steel
in the streets
by night
and
Black love songs
at dawn.

Maxine Hall Elliston

For Gwen

A great writer, I believe it was Hemingway, once said writers, at least great writers, never receive any recognition while they live, or something like that. Well my poem expresses my sentiments about that exactly.

Pulitzer prizes, lavish appointments, laurels

                                       everywhere.

Speeches, banquets, letters

                                     the regular fare.

It must be a great and wonderful feeling,

                                living but still there.

January 8, 1969

Live Celebration
For Gwendolyn Brooks,
on her birthday, June 1968

Tight grip
but loose
reins hold
in harness
this teeming
Tribe-of-
Gwen

And a seeming
almost
careless
watchful gaze
that does not
dull the
captives'
vision.

Love, laughter
light the
highly humid
summer night
in old "Chi";

radiate
a warmth
which, at another
season,
is enough
to thaw
the chilling
hawk.

Tonight,
it is a
June birth
we celebrate,
a lush green
life.

A guitar
plucks a
happy note
and lyric voices
resound, affirming
beauty in a shared
black world.

You in your
quiet grace,
the face imprinted
on the OBAC
wall of respect,
act as if you
do not know it is you
they serenade.

Lovestruck,
your words
delivered: received
are fashioned
by the now
generation
into your
gift of

new
song.

Bronzeville Breakthrough
For Gwendolyn Brooks,
Poet Laureate, Illinois

Real.
Cool.
The Real
thing
We are
And you—
giving us
the courage
to be
real
while we
grow
steadily
strong,
beaneating
with Sadie
and Maud,
De Witt Williams,
and those
nameless
Black
heroes.

Growing
stronger,
Oakener,
with you
and those
Oaken Reeds,
Oakener
each day

like
reeds
tossed
in life/death
by the
furious
winds of
our times—
always
the tempest
for us,
for the few
who are
not afraid
of "No,"
a breakthrough
into
Yes.

What you
gave was
beauty,
Black beauty.
You saw
the beauty
of the Sundays
of Satin Legs
and all
his put-ons
of lotion,
lavender and
pine oil—
those styles

and scents
and ego feats,
those necessary
trips in
compensation
for those
Oh-so-many-
put-downs,
deprivations,
flowing
bitter
from too-scant
mother's milk,
too few desserts,
too many butt
spanks, grumpy,
bumpy-mattressed
sleep
of cold-wintered
starless
nights.
Yes, give
Satin Legs
his senses
and his scents
soul meats at
"Joe's Eats."
Give him back
his jazz and
his sculpture
and his art.

Being.

Just being,
in the squalor
of our world
and Time,
Nothing
but a plain
Black boy
is deserving
of a purple
heart
for valor
and remembrance
with the lean
face indelibly
imprinted on
our walls of
R-E-S-P-E-C-T.

And Trouble
in Bronzville,
in the Mecca,
in South Side
Kitchenettes,
comes stalking
dead-end streets,
unannounced by
"gold-flecked
beautiful banner."
Trouble is
the Washerwoman's
blues,
Staggerlee's
Stormy Monday

Blues,
The Lonesome
Blues, The
Weary Blues,
the low-down-
funky-bring-'em-
right-on-down-
to-the-real-
nitty gritty
blues.

Tea
is nothing
more than
tea; and
there ain't
no bread and
Life is the
Supreme
effort of
paying one's
dues on a
day-to-day
credit plan,
trying to
live,
trying to dodge
those
deathly
games
fixed
by the man.

Black chaos
hawked in the
windy grays
of hopeless days.
One mother bends,
kissing her
stilled
"killed boy"
and another
and another
and another
enter
the womanhood
throwing
parting kisses
of goodbye
to early
killed dreams,
vacant lots,
abortions
which are
not so soon
forgotten
by the mother.

And yet.
And yet
we must
forget and
forget and
begin
to
Be,

now.

And
in the end
as it was
before
so many
blindingly
bleak
times before,
we find a
job that's
just begun.
For only
the likes
of you,
at this late
hour,
can show
us how to be,
Be
Cool
Real
Cool
Be Real.
Cool.

Hoyt W. Fuller

Lost Moment
Some thoughts on the occasion of a tribute to Gwen

When it is all over
when we have stomped our feet
and shook our fists
and moaned in wordless bitterness
like choruses of cadavers robed in gloom
when we have drained ourselves of rage
and stand silent and impotent
alone
will we know at last
will we understand
that passion builds no bridges
that rhetoric is no music
that pain is not panacea nor power
        though it teaches spirit
        and defines the god in man
will we see, will we know
that evil is a solid thing
real like iron
that it bends and breaks
only when the strength of fire
the weight of worlds
conspire to confront it?

When it is ended—
this bombast and this bluff—
will we move quietly then
into the shadows
out in the storm
into the sea
will we finally seek the wisdom
and like wise children
hold hands against the dark?

This crime we would commit
against our beauty
this crime of eloquence and fear
against our children
will doom us
to walk the empty plains of hell
forever and ever
more.

December 31, 1969

Zack Gilbert

For Gwendolyn Brooks

Queen of your craft, queen
Of the perfect word and shorthand phrase,
The neat punch lines that sweetly amaze
The most dubious.

You stand alone
In your ingenious role,
Your images are sharp and deft,
Your symbols bold,
Your intent fierce and clear,
And yet a softness there
Mellows the cold heart.

Queen of your craft,
Noble poetess.

For Gwendolyn Brooks *I wrote about five years ago, and the other [p. 47]*
I wrote recently. Z. G.

When I Heard Dat White Man Say

When I heard dat
      White man say on radio
Duh uder day,
"Gwen Brooks don broke
Wid der establishment. Don
Got in der black militant camp."
I said, "You faggot fool,
Where you think she been all der time?
'Cause she use what you call
Good English don mean she aint
      Black.
There's uh lotta them like that
Going 'round fooling you, baby.
          An you better believe it.

for gwendolyn brooks
a "note of love"

brooks start with cloud condensation
allah crying
for his lost children

brooks babble
from mountain tops to settle
in collecting the earth's essence

pure spring fountain
of love/knowledge
for those who find
and dare drink
of it

September 23, 1969

Words
for Gwen Brooks

Word like the earth/
Creating/
rain-word/ Dawn-word/
Strength in your heart
where it always was anyway/
Words like 50 million strong Black people
moving for a nation.

        /is her strength.

Her word
is her work.
Keep it.
Her strength
is yours, and yours is hers in her word,
if you keep it.

Madimba: Gwendolyn Brooks
Music is its own heartbeat

Double-conscious sister in the veil,
Double-conscious sister in the veil;
Double-conscious sister in the veil:
Double-conscious sister in the veil.

You beat out the pulse with your mallets,
the brown wishbone anemones
unflowered & unworn in Chicago congo
prints, images, otherness, images

from the fossilbank: Madimba
Black man; I'm a black man; black—
A-um-ni-pad-me-hum—
another brother gone:

"the first act of liberation
is to destroy one's cage"—
a *love supreme;*
a *love supreme.*

Images: words: language
typing the round forms: Juneteenth,
baby, we free, free at last:
black man, I'm a black man.

A garden is a manmade vision,
rectangular, weeded, shelled,
pathed, hosed, packed in,
covered with manure, pruned;

I own you; you're mine, you
mine, baby: to bear unborn things.

Double-conscious sister in the veil:
Double-conscious sister in the veil.

Black woman: America is artful
outside time, ideal outside space;
you its only machine: Madimba:
Double-conscious sister in the veil.

a gathering of artists
for gwendolyn brooks . . . in remembrance of a party she gave.

seemingly,
i shall never
forget this night
listening to u
beautiful creatures
of pied-less beauty
cursing and arguing
at
    one
         an/other fool jumps-up and says,
shit hell godamn
universal niggers humanity
shit what about humanity.

and art
still remaining calm
under this
hypersensitive
tonic individuals who are
BLACK AND BEAUTIFUL
love to love.

i
love to love freely
your smooth voice
with arrogant tones
sweeping impatient rhythms into
my naked-ear
and the smell
of scotch on
your breath is
ART

in its natural form.

what makes (them me
me them
us we)
and i use
these damn meaningless pronouns at a time like this.
new sentences are born a new man is discovered a
new art nurtured in us
cause we are a beautiful people
with scotch & water
pleasing each other
we kiss & continue to curse on the rug of no mannerism.
tell me what
did you say
            a-b-o-u-t-b-l-a-c-k-w-o-m-a-n-h-o-o-d

and my senses became
one with yours
and here i go again
getting into
non sensual pronouns,
but baby
ain't we real tonite
real again
real alive
us all and other pronouns
we are crazy
maniacs
us
all
in
the

same
damn boat
but
free
all up in heah
at this
BLACK GATHERING OF ARTISTS.

August 28, 1967

some smooth lyrics for a natural people

clever mother
mother of divine cleverness
grandmother
rocking rocking
rocking to rhythms that exist in the talking sea of unchange
humming humming
humhumhumhumhumhumhummmmmmmmmmmmmmmm
rocking back and forth
on porches that under&overstand.

smooth amber lyrics of
a faith in the unknown
a known faith of peace wisdoms
peace wisdoms
peace wisdoms
PEACE WISDOMS.

none of US never committed suicide baby!
pressures of society's life are on each of US
i know
i can feel
with u we
both feel together
but what is it that keeps us from
JUMPING! JUMPING!
off
off
into
the can and containers
of physical space.

clever mother
mother of divine cleverness

grandmother
rocking
and humming
humminghummmmmmmmmmmmm
rocking back and forth
on porches that under&overstand.

could it be the power
of OUR GRANDMOTHER'S rocking
could it be the power
of OUR GRANDMOTHER'S remedystocureillnesses

could it be the power
of OUR GRANDMOTHER'S
smooth lyrics
or the unchanged ideas of an
ancient african&africanamerican wisdom
that has been passed down & has
penetrated deep into their
souls & our souls alike
hummmmmmmmmmmmmmmmmmmmmmmmmmmmm.

smooth
some smooth lyrics for a natural people
a people of nature
a people of persons
a people of human beings
whose self is a live
in each of us
whose quality of self
makes us a complete and total people
nature has proven that we are
not a warring people

we are not a killing people
but a peacepeople a lovinglong people
who can hold
hands with the moon & sun
without getting chilledorsunburned
who can reach beneath
the depths of the earth
without
technological devices to sooth the ills
of natural people only.

clever mother
mother of divine cleverness
grandmother
keep rocking and humming hummmmmmmmmmms
of humanness.

The Tree Poem
parable for/of Sister Gwendolyn

and our tree grew as trees do
(up)
but, when the others had leaves of heat
she sun-stretched with naked arms
and beat the tall grass for the love,
while others' leaves rotted golden red
hers scorched greener than ever
in camouflage to bring back the head of the lion,
while the others were bare in the warmth of winters
·she bore the fruits of purple passion
making love like a queen.
and this is not unnatural,
but supernatural

for we shall know them by their progeny.

Raymond A. Joseph

our meeting

/

for Gwen Brooks

since our meeting in the mecca,
gray mind-cells have grown
deep/rich black & filled with fresh air—
waiting to erupt creating
scenes of maleness black stampedes & walls.
though they struggle still in swimming
                  now survive!
& resist
            the bleaching waves
            in that "universal" sea of dying
            weak/sick phagocytes.

November 6 1969

Three Poems for Gwendolyn Brooks

1. Sketch

Is the moment conscious that (with public prescription)

> Black Runnymedes
> and murdered hope
> stretched to the root of my thumbs

tranquilized strokes any sleep

> with holy pits of memory
> like yesterday's dying. . . .
> Shoveled into my loin

like lions, crust with Black men's grief,

> this grief: the howl from mocking rain and gritty sun
> and runny haze like pus; my crisp and sudden summer
> blooms in syllables of blood. . . .

and lies humped in my house with a grunt of history

2. The agony and the bone

Chicago shanks . . . . .
>   hung along the lake
>   like churches; the rib awake

>   the groin of fasted days
>   for Lazaruses raised
>   from shanty towns, a phrase

of her like stitching wounds can make;

raw, the freshly killed alone
    the young obscenity of !

       weening in the streets
       the sacrificial bleats
       of slaughters, meats

for mayors. She like love: the agony and the bone

3. Interview in color

Did poetry
choose you
or was it
the other way
through?
And if so
where did
the two
of you
meet—
on a
vermilion street
near the
South Side El
or taupe
in pain
where *Endymion*
fell?

For Eusi, Ahy Kwei & Gwen Brooks

In us and into us and ours
This movement rises every day
As the day whose fire informs
The rhythm of the sons who must live
After the death of those familiar faces.

We move from origin,
The singular fruit, at times bitter
As the Sophiatown winters we did not create,
To roots, stronger than the grief
Which groans under the weighted
Centuries of systematic rape and ruin.

We move from origin to roots.
Past the rancid face of anger and sorrow
Where I was a stranger to my breath
Rests the color of my eye
Calling my name
In the depths that reclaim
My pulse in the darknesses that alone
Remember the face of the warrior
Whose name knows a multiple doom
Before he is born to follow the eye
To the shapes remembered where the spirit moves
On to the darknesses the eye caresses
In us and into us and ours.

Helen H. King

For Gwendolyn Brooks

The eye that pierces
With wide precision—
Then clicks
Past the molten agonies
To the divine question.
Sets a taut, black lip
Against the circumstance
With eagle's beak and wing of hawk
Beats incessantly
At the crusted wound
Demands the sullen purity
Behind the sound of 'El'
Pool hall, amens and ashen child
And neither sleeps
Nor loves, nor laughs
Nor sips of wine
In forgetfulness
But swipes ever
At the sutured spirit
Of Blackness.

June 1970

The Sun Came

And if sun comes
How shall we greet him?
    —Gwendolyn Brooks

The sun came, Miss Brooks—
After all the night years.
He came spitting fire from his lips.
And we flipped—We goofed the whole thing.
It looks like our ears were not equipped
For the fierce hammering.

And now the Sun has gone, has bled red
Weeping behind the hills.
Again the night year shadows form.
The rays of Red have pierced the deep, have struck
The core. We cannot sleep.
The shadows sing: Malcolm, Malcolm, Malcolm
The darkness ain't like before.

The Sun came, Miss Brooks
And we goofed the whole thing.
I think
(Though ain't no vision visited my cell.)

To Gwendolyn Brooks

O Courier on Pegasus. O Daughter of Parnassus!
O splendid woman of the purple stick.

When beaten and blue, despairingly we sink
Within obfuscating mire,
Oh, cradle in your bosom us, hum your lullabies
And soothe our souls with kisses of verse
That stir us on to search for light.

O Mother of the world. Effulgent lover of the Sun!
Forever speak the truth.

His body is an Eloquence
Every Negro has something to say. Simply because he is a Negro. . . . His mere body . . . is an eloquence.—Gwendolyn Brooks

But in the saying
let not despair
cast its shadow
nor hate stifle the tongue.

(Wailing, fullness of breast,
passing from the lung
plummeting
to the melting sun.

Screeching of the midnight beast
against the midnight skin of steel.

Trombones of lost hope.
Bones of quivering song
dashed, dashed, dashed skyward.

Indignities we've all known,
hoary laughter clutching
at the loins.)

"His mere body is an eloquence."

swaying in foreboding winds,
ascending not ungraciously.

singing the blues, spirituals,
honky-tonk jazz,
songs of black bards
leaning on the common
ground of the burning past.

This day
This night
This eloquence of sorrow
This robe of innocence
This shroud of guilt
This canopy of flaming ice
This sea
    This sky
        This sun.

Gwendolyn Brooks

she doesn't wear
costume jewelry
& she knew that walt disney
was/is making a fortune off
false-eyelashes and that time magazine is the
authority on the knee/grow.
her makeup is total-real.

a negro english instructor called her:
     "a fine negro poet."
a whi-te critic said:
     "she's a credit to the negro race."
somebody else called her:
     "a pure negro writer."
johnnie mae, who's a senior in high school said:
     "she & langston are the only negro poets we've
     read in school and i understand her."
pee wee used to carry one of her poems around in his
    back pocket;
     the one about being cool. that was befo pee wee
     was cooled by a cop's warning shot.

into the sixties
a word was born . . . . BLACK
& with black came poets
& from the poets' ball points came:
black doubleblack purpleblack blueblack beenblack was
black daybeforeyesterday blackerthan ultrablack super
black blackblack yellowblack niggerblack blackwhi-te-
    man
blackerthanyoueverbes ¼ black unblack coldblack clear
black my momma's blackerthanyourmomma pimpleblack
    fall

black so black we can't even see you black on black in
black by black technically black mantanblack winter
black coolblack 360degreesblack coalblack midnight
black black when it's convenient rustyblack moonblack
black starblack summerblack electronblack spaceman
black shoeshineblack jimshoeblack underwearblack ugly
black auntjimammablack, uncleben'sriceblack willie best
black unsubstance black
black blackisbeautifulblack I justdiscoveredblack negro

and everywhere the
lady "negro poet"
appeared the poets were there.
they listened & questioned
& went home feeling uncomfortable/unsound & so-
        untogether
they read/re-read/wrote & re-wrote
& came back the next time to tell the
lady "negro poet"
how beautiful she was/is & how she had helped them
& she came back with:
        how necessary they were and how they've helped her.
the poets walked & as space filled the vacuum between
        them & the
lady "negro poet"
u could hear one of the blackpoets say:
        "bro, they been callin that sister by the wrong name."

David Llorens

Of a Woman Who Turns Rivers

Males carry the
hormones that
do the work
I'm told.
Can a man
make a woman
who can
make a man?
She called a
young dude
gentle once
and made him
hope he really
is.
She called a
young dude
scholar once
and made him
hope to someday
be.
A man helped
make a woman
who helped
make a man
who loves
that woman.
If she ever call
him a bad
muthafuckah,
watch out,
'cause *Our* Miss Brooks do not lie.

James C. Morris

"Ruby-jane, Mother-wife"
After reading A Song in the Front Yard, *by G. Brooks*

(She leaps still after happiness
in a flaming, flowered dress.)
Wearing colors dead and drab
may speak well for home or lab,
may be fine for Jenni Lee—
but not for me.
Jenni doesn't feel compelled
to taste of water undistilled,
or stick ringed finger in the fire,
tang-whet her lips with sharp desire;
black-laced leg and shouldered fur
may not be at all for her.
But there's music in *my* veins,
undiluted jazz-built strains,
moonlight on Jamaican seas,
stolen magic among the Hebrides.
Too bad, husband, devoted child,
that your mother-wife's so wild.
Don't stare at me with eyes askance
if I shake my hips to dance,
if I run off with life next door—
what's his music calling for?
Better let me leap this stile,
and mourn me with a noonday smile.

October 24, 1969

Rukudzo Murapa

Gwen Brooks—Our Inspirer

Gwendolyn Brooks
A smashing Black she-figure
Calm are her looks
Yet the dimensions of her gift are bigger
Sustained by a bottomless pool of honesty.

Gwen Brooks
    That is her name
Unmeasurable is her fame
Yet her modesty remains the same.

She is the poet-laureate of Illinois
But for us she is bigger
A no nigger

She is the poet-laureate of the Black World.
When she writes "For Malcolm"
You feel it and miss him
When she writes of "The Wall of Respect"
You respect the wall of our heroes
When she writes "We Cool"
You know, her gift is a never-drying pool.

Gwen Brooks
    That is her name
She reads but never screams
Yet the flow of her words—a delicious cream.

Paul Dunbar, Conrad Rivers, Leopold Senghor,
Claude McKay, Langston Hughes, W. E. B. Du Bois
These form her class. Dedicated to the service
of her people, she never tires.

Right on Gwen,

Keep on keeping on.

Our inspirer
Thanks Gwen.

A Jive Eschatology
we have always been at war. . . Max Stanford

It is night, and like the others, I clean my weapons,
sitting under the raw red doom of a blood sucking moon.

It is all so familiar. I know that my father
and his father have gone this route before.
I know that sometimes, I am merely the mirror
of someone else's murders
of someone else's neck twisted,
turning in the eye bulging wind.

All of our prophets have come up shaky,
the avenues run blood.
days like these, we know that there is no hope,
or at least none that we can touch.

All of the old ways are dead or dying;
and this is as it should be—
rotting scriptures crumble in mythic cellars
so
we beat our drums
adorn ourselves in bright
robes and enter palaces of flesh
and enter halls of killer dreams
and sink ghoulishly into blood crimes.

Minds buckle beneath the arctic horrors.
all of the savannahs have been chilled
by the pale plundering christians.
It is so familiar, Daddy knew
and kept his piece handy.

I am a young man, somewhat skinny/

I would rather sing and fuck women
would rather love my children, yet unborn.
would rather wizard them with green images
would rather dance and be space/motion
than kill any man;
even though I know killing
is also part of the timeless pattern of things.

But seas and the world's vermin
swim in me; yeah, we are polluted
sinews and a horror as old as rock
haunts us.
that is why orgasm is mixed vision:
birth/death, the joy yell when sperm first asserts itself,
then retreats, fleeing from the cold north winds.

It was first fist, then rock, then missiles, then the bullet;
the circling birds turned into atomic bombers—
the energy of fire, once holy, became the holocaust
of nagasaki's flash death.
this . . . this . . . this speck
this . . . this . . . this speck hung in endless space.

2
When Europe left the caves,
    it reached its cultural apex
with the perfection of murder;
Sir Walter Raleigh ran slaves
in honor of art.

King Leopold
slept on piles of Congo bodies,
his excellency, a meat freak.

a cast of clowns
and regal faggots crowd the white man's
history.

and down the long tunnel, the unfulfilled, the unavenged
stumble/crawl wailing for their various gods.

Men have killed in the name of rock.
Men have killed in the name of God.
Men have killed in the name of land.
Men have killed in the name of Allah.
Men have killed in the name of Shatan.
Men have killed in the name of pussy.
Men have killed in the name of honor.
Men have killed in the name of peace.
Do I need to go on?

The weapons are oiled, polished, gaunt, ready;
and in a flash, I see the face of my intended victims.

Tejumola Ologboni

to Gwen
and her new natural

her mind
was always nappy
been makin
us
feel natural
for years

small
gentle,
a smile
you feel
she real

whose words
TOWER
like a Black
Giant
catching David's
pebbles
laying them back
in the brook

She Black
(a smile)
you feel
she real

Bronzeville Poet
For Gwendolyn Brooks

The streets of Bronzeville
seem more beautiful
because you gave them honesty.
Made Philistine experiences
more than monotonous copy
for obituary columns.
Helped black children
realize that filth and
dilapidated houses aren't
the only world they have.
That blackness is more than
being able to recite black poetry
or wearing a voluminous natural.
You gave them fertile
soil from Africa to
scrub their faces.
Lifted their pregnable hearts
when racist institutions
branded their minds
with inferior images.
And the clumsy tongues of
button down collar bureaucrats
told them that America
was the black man's salvation.

The streets of Bronzeville
seem more beautiful.
The blues at Pepper's Lounge
begin to take on
greater significance.
Muddy Waters becomes
a living legend and even

first graders admire Otis Redding.
The shadows under the "el" tracks
along 63rd still hold fond memories,
of glittering neon lights
and mellifluous music.
And when we listen carefully
the buried sounds of the Savoy
Ballroom can be heard over the clamor
of screeching jitnies and street
corner sermons.
And though Michigan Ave. has
lost its aristocracy,
a few buildings remain
that have survived "mecca's" fate
And the dingy food shack
on 35th is not forgotten
amidst the neo-technology
of industrialized war schools.
Its hickory aroma
trickles to the corner
newsstand where two retired
postal workers see their dreams
absorbed by a dusty checker board.
And senile women with their
moth-eaten shopping bags,
searching for bargains at
the catholic salvage store
aren't to be damned for blasphemy.
And the new black poets
begin to talk about
creating something
revolutionary . . .
black life styles/

and relevant dialogue/
They take a walk
through your Bronzeville
and begin to discover themselves.
See true images/the gut of life
silhouetted against the transparent
fabric of the black experience.
A Blues Singer greets them
and fiddles on his twelve string guitar,
while little Bronzeville children listen
and dance to your poetry.

October 3 1969

Sterling D. Plumpp

Black Angel Child

Her eyes, marvelous sunrises.

She flies
She flies
    away from us
With our steel-accustomed ways
Of making beautiful days die
Like the inadequacy of silent symphonies.

Her light hangs in her motions.

She flies
She flies
    through many dreams
We have buried deep in our dead
And decaying memories of what
Life should've been to living men.

Her smile deifies setting souls.

She flies
She flies
    into aesthetic fountains
Where human aspirations like pearls
Are made precious monuments of delight
By the aching desire to edit all wrongs.

Her whole being is a rebirth.

She flies
She flies
    Black Angel Child flies . . .
Flies beyond time's limiting province
But perpetually reaches back to us, mortals,
Seeking immortality in our pursuit of beauty.

On Getting an Afro
For Gwendolyn Brooks

She didn't know she was beautiful.
Though her smiles were dawn,
her voice was bells,
and her skin deep velvet Night.

She didn't know she was beautiful.
Although her deeds,
kind, generous, unobtrusive,
gave hope to some,
and help to others,
and inspiration to us all. (And
beauty is as beauty does,
they say.)

Then one day there blossomed
a crown upon her head,
bushy, bouffant, real Afro-down—
Queen Nefertété again.
And now her regal wooly crown
declares,
"I know
I'm black
AND
beautiful."

To gwendolyn brooks
The creator
In the beginning—words

Words massing images of sacred exclusion
Glacial crust words unfeeling untouching unmeaning

Blacks plucked from their Edens
Listened for the silenced drumbeat

And then propelled by the absent heartbeat
She climbed into the chilling vacuum
Soared above the dawning ether
and descended
        THEN THERE WAS LIFE
That smelled of ham hocks 'n greens
Cloroxed sheets flapping on blue Mondays
Minds unfettered, screams narrowed and Miles blew his horn
      And NOW THERE'S INFINITY
That follows the "L" tracks, the black greenless jungles to new nations
Nations not conceived in Genesis and not to die in Revelations

to Gwen,
  mo luv

if i were a painter
  it would be easier
i suppose
   though paint i know
has its limitations.
     how do you paint
  the pulse
    or mix the essence of
    the tender heart
what color is love, throbbing
  through the black veins.

if i were a musician,
    perhaps
i
 could write a score
    with notes
  and special combinations
advanced sounds, beyond directions
  or, you could hear
a voice ringing around the air
  heavy, vibrato with encouragement

jazz timing at the throat
     or i could beat drums
  and you would hear
     but
what is the beat of care,
how rolls the rhythm of tender

  if i were a painter
  if i were a musician

                i could
                maybe, but
            being the poet
                            only
            and knowing that luv
            has its way of choking around the mind
            which is somehow connected to
                    these fingers
            that make sounds on paper and because
        the sounds are not the words and the words are not
                    who you are
        and description is afterall useless if i can not
                    de tail you Black Woman
                        you our Sister
                        you who i call a Lady

    you are the song that Billie
            was born into singing
    you are the picture that Black
            people eternal go on painting
    true, you are love & lovelier & lovingest
            all that we be and are yet to become
    you are mo luv and mo luv and mo luv and mo luv and mo luvvvvvv

sunday/evening at gwen's

and we came that sun   day
etheridge &
                    i to that
quiet / looooking / at
                         that held
a blk/
        woman / poet's
  thots
                and we came
that sun
      day & saw her
naturaaal
            beauty. so quiet. but
full of fire
                when it bees necessary.
& we came that day
                    to read our work
but left
        knooowing
                    hers.

we a bad people
for gwendolyn brooks
    a fo real bad one

i mean.
          we bees real
bad.
        we gots bad songs
sung on every station
we gots some bad   NATURALS
on our heads
              and brothers gots
so   bad loud   (fo real)
     dashiki   threads
              on them.
                          i mean when
we dance   u know we be doooing it
                        when we walk
                        we be doooing it
            when we rap
            we be doooing it
                    and
when we love.   well.   yeah.   u be knowing
bout that too.   (uh-huh!)
                          we got some BAAD
thots and actions
                    like off those white mothafuckas
                    and rip it off if it ain't nailed
                    down and surround those white/
                    knee/grow/pigs & don't let them
                    live to come back again into
                    our neighborhoods (we ain't
                    no museum for white/
                    queer/minds/dicks to
                    fuck us up)

and we be gitting into a
SPIRITUAL thing.
                    like discipline
of the mind,
                    no drinking cept to celebrate
our victories/births.
                    no smoking.   no shooting
needles into our blk/veins
                              full of potential blk/
gold cuz our
            high must come from
                          thinking working
                          planning fighting loving
                          our blk/selves
                                      into nationhood.
i mean.
        when we spread ourselves thin over our
        land and see our young/ warriors/
        sisters moving/ running on blk/
        hills of freedom.
                      we'll boo   ga   loo
in love.
        aaa-ee-ooo-wah/   wah
        aaa-ee-ooo-wah/   wah
        aaa-ee-ooo-wah/   wah
        aaa-ee-ooo-wah/   wah
        git em with yo bad self. don.   rat now.
        go on & do it. dudley.   rat now.   yeah.
        run it on down.   gwen. rat now. yeah.   yeah.
        aaa-e-oooooo. wah / wah.
        aaa-e-oooooo. wah / wah.
        We a BAAAD people.
                        & we be getting
              BAAAADER
                        every day.

for gwen—

because of
beauty.
life.
example. &
need—
in more than
gratitude and
appreciation
but with
love
sharon.

This Is For You

This is for you. This is what you've always been
A poem whose name begins and ends with the words
"This is for you."
You stand like a fine brownstone sturdy, tall . . .
Embracing all your people.
You endure the countless things they do inside
Your veins . . . the shouting, the yelling, rope jumping
The loving . . . and you protect them in the shadows of the
Stairwells in the corridors of your heart . . . because they are
Of you.
Your paint is chipped, they mark your walls . . . the one
On the first floor hall has in big black letters
"BLACK IS BEAUTIFUL," "COME TO JESUS," and in the back
Up on the fifth floor . . . "IT'S SO BEAUTIFUL TO BE BLACK,"
                    signed . . . "Pepita"
Inside you the bean eaters laugh and cry . . . worry and grin . . .
And in 201 is Floyd, who learned early on the block to
                    cut school . . .
                    shoot pool . . .
                    thin gin . . .
This is for you . . . for all the years . . . your patience, love,
The silent tears you cried.
The sounds of Miles, Lady Day, and Mamie Smith come out
Of 318.
Among all this you stand like a fine brownstone
Elegant, serene . . . a poem . . .
                    a poem . . .
That says to everyone . . . "This is for you."

A.B. Spellman

Song For the Sisters

as much as my eyes
may be said to be open
it was you who opened them.
as much as my mind
may be said to be clean
you cleansed it.

i entered the world
with a scream my sister
that you called a prayer.
you loved & you made me
you suffered & saved me
so that life is you, sister
& strength is you, sister
& growth & survival & truth
are you, sister.

& when i think god thoughts
the earth's femininity opens
& when i think man thoughts
the city explodes into stone.
& then i see world thoughts
& black men start dying
for living.

i return to you

& you bid me move

& i move . . . movement moves

& black controls.

as much as my eyes
may be said to be doors
you walk into them.
as much as my mind
may be said to be space
you filled it.

i can see worlds
thru the eyes of your womb.
white death cannot enter
that room.

black woman.

prentiss taylor jr.

/from an 18 year old poet with a raggedy face

                                       i shall tell my son one day
how my granpa found so much solace
back down south, from sitting on the front step he made his own self
stroking his sparse whiskers   and gazing way up yonder
seeing beyond the horizon of time.

"my father inherited his father's hair
but thicker—a richer harvest of wisdom, and many nights when i would
    ask him
a particularly trying question
he would be silent as his hand confered with his chin,   as if
he were reading an ancestral braille. i waited reverently and was
    answered
and all was made plain.

"and this a here,"   i will then say
"is my wild and most holy shrine. each
convoluted hair is a LIVING projection
of our people's experience.
"on this hair   is written: 'ohnedaruth'   you can't
see it, but feel it there."   i another in my fingers play
"ah. on this   'sundiata of mali' is inscribed.
"and this suppleone which refuses to stop growing as it winds its way
touching and intertwining with many others!   it is marked, simply:
                                       gwen brooks
catching his boyish chin in my hands,   i shall tell my son one day
to learn to cultivate his coming consciousness.
              and he will smile, nodding quietly.
              as young chieftains always   do.

A Significant Other

Gwendolyn Brooks, you *are* unique.
Not conservative, bigoted, super
Black and ultra hipped, but sleek,
And so beautifully at ease, you slip
Into one's mind and heart
Before one can injunction the start
Of it all.

If I fall
In love with your congeniality
It will be the beneficial reality
Of my awe for overt black sincerity.

If I could absorb the tranquility
        of your heart;
It would be the end of my hostility
        and my start
To dismiss the equivocation of my destiny.

I would proclaim it my planet
To zealously follow it.
No more procrastination,
Fear of social retaliation.
Just my star
And my realization
That my life
Is not mine only.

For Gwen—1969

The slender, shy, and sensitive young girl
is woman now,
her words a power in the Ebon land.
Outside her window on the street
a mass of life moves by.
Chicago is her city.
Her heart flowers with its flame—
Old stockyards, new beaches
all the little store-front churches
and the bar on the corner.
Dreamer and seer of tales
she witnesses rebellion,
struggles and sweat.
The people are her heartbeat—
In their footsteps pulsate daily
all her black words of fire and blood.

Black Consciousness
Gwendolyn Brooks

Reachin into the depth of
                    the Blk Man's Soul,
With your sense of logical
                    perspective.
    Your worth to us
Far more than the
                    cracker's/gold.
Acting as the stabilizer of
                    our BLK/action.
Bringing with you the
                    cradle/civilization.
Nurture of the creative
                    BLK/Gods.
                    provider of the sexuality
that will always be yours.
                    mover of/freedom,
relater of truth/wisdom.
How best do we describe you?
    Woman of the Nile/Backbone of the
Overseas/African
                    BLK pearl/gold?
Why not Blk/Woman.

w. d. wandick

for the honeybee Queen and her poets

it's four-forty in the morning,
outside the wind blows heaving the greenbunched leaves
back and forth like the breasts of some big-bosomed woman.
marvin gaye is busy thinkin' 'bout his baby
and this wideeyed lady laying on my desk, natural haired,
grinning her original brooks upside down grin
compels me to sleeplessness and exhortation

hey lady!
you better copyright those eyes!
that group! those poets!
the latimore! the rodgers! the davis! and the cook!
it was a mad session, gotta get it outa my veins!
baby, my true purpose is to sing to dance and this insomniac
moment. i gladly sing you and dance that group.
they must be kissed and supplicated with more than meetings
more than feelings, with something like a glazed word,
immortal and forbidden, yet needed.
gwen, the pulsings from this jumping heart scream like a child
somewhere in every ghetto under ten above eight mainly black
definitely high,
"once upon a reincarnated time you were the responsive Word,
a reigning Queen, a honeybee Queen. you are stinging me!
and that group of beepoets! damn them!
god like santa claus might not exist but there
                ARE
          black people."

kids,
for you the rhythm of my feet and body singing in dance a hymn
in and out between trees and on the tops of these green windblown
    leaves,
i shall for you caress the caressing cold wind.

you know, and warm that wind—THAT'S WHAT WE ARE,
THAT'S   WHAT   BLACKNESS   IS—IT'S HEAT!
it warms cold things.
it lights dark places, like white/black, black/white,
black/black, white/white minds: we are praise, sisters.
                                    we are love, brothers.
                                    we are frighteningly real
like the honeybee Queen's smiling eyes and unique mouth.

hey lady!
i still can't sleep. even if i turn you face down on my desk,
i would still see you.
i would still see you.
i would still see intoxicating Kindness killing sleep.

Gwen Brooks, A Pyramid

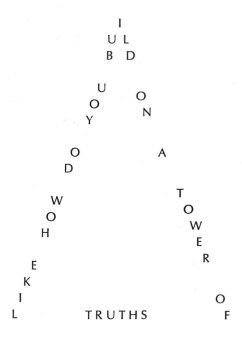

Sigemonde Kharlos Wimberli

Drum Song Sister
For Gwendolyn Brooks

Our drums were ripped,
forbidden,
long before we knew
how precious our drums really were
But you kept the song
You never lost the throbbing
pulsebeat of the ancient theme.
Nodrums nodrums nodrums
No drums,
'til you.
'Til you revived
the spirit deep and true
of who and what and where
we are and from and do(ing)
You
became the throbbing pulse
across the vastness,
span between our selfhood and our usness
Nodrums nodrums nodrums
We had no drums
'Til you
'Til you reverberated
drumbeat songs
our heads pulsed through our hands
'Til you
our lines, our lives
were searching veins
for bloodbeat chanting
You are our song,
our bloodbeat chanting,
Love,
whose throbbing trueness

warmly fills
the chasm between hopeful heart
and striving hand.
You are our song
our bloodbeat chanting
our chanting bloodbeat
Our beat yours, your beat ours
You are our drum song sister.

December 28, 1969

FICTION

A White Loaf of Bread

TO GWENDOLYN BROOKS, QUEEN OF POETS, QUEEN OF WOMEN,
QUEEN OF ALL OUR INSPIRATIONS AND OUR ASPIRATIONS.
AND TO
all Black mothers everywhere, including my mother and my wife, Grace,
and my daughter, Barbara, and to Margaret Walker Alexander. To the
struggle against a white establishment which, for nearly four hundred
years, has tried, deliberately and diabolically, to make Black men into
women and Black women into men. May the white establishment's fail-
ure be eternal, through our Black deeds and Black efforts.

His mother wasn't his mother anymore.

His mother was a traitor. That's all there was to it, don't care how sweet she had been to him, ever since she sold him down the river to the white folks.

Robby Youngblood sat on the trunk of an old oak tree watching the other kids play "Ten Ten Double Ten" in a vacant lot over near Ida Mae Raglin's house. It was the Spring of 1932, and yesterday the world had been cold and ugly and naked and lonely-looking, but That Man Up There had worked hard all night long with his giant paint brush dripping with light green paint and now the world of Crossroads, Georgia was togged out in a pretty, bright and shiny green. But let it be spring or winter, or summertime or fall, it didn't make any never mind, his mother was a traitor. Damn her soft-faced, sweet-talking soul.

An unconscious frown creased his wide handsome forehead as he watched Ida Mae as she leaned against a chinaberry tree with her face hidden in the circle of her arms. She was IT. TEN TEN DOUBLE TEN. FORTY-FIVE FIFTEEN. Robby's dark narrow eyes idled nervously at the round calves of her long brown legs and the hollow in the back of her knees and as far up on her thighs as the hem of her gingham dress reached. She was his girl, really his girl, and he certainly was her feller.

And it wasn't puppy love either—it was the real doggone thing. He felt funny watching her on the sly like this. A strange taste in his mouth which he kept swallowing and collecting again and a warmth all over his restless body and a brand new sharp smell in his nostrils. Ida Mae hadn't seen him yet, he thought. Her voice sang out in a high soprano, sometimes clear, sometimes the words running together—it didn't make him any never mind.

> TEN TEN DOUBLE TEN
> FORTY-FIVE FIFTEEN
> HONEY IN THE BEE FA
> I CAN'T SEE YA
> ALL HID DEE—

He watched the kids scampering to their hiding places, as he sat there throwing rocks at an old tin can about fifteen feet away. The ridges of the tree trunk nibbled at his nervous backside. He didn't feel like playing anything, and yet he did not feel like going home where his mother always was. Especially today, when he was bubbling over with a brand new kind of restlessness. All day long. Just as jumpy as a crazy grasshopper. Coming from his after-school job in the suburbs he hadn't been able to get his mind off of Mama and what she used to be to him and what they used to be to each other, but even now, almost four months after it had happened, he always worked up a violent anger against her whenever he thought about it. He had lived it over and over again. Many many times. He had dreamed about it even.

Ever since he could remember she had taught him and his sister to stand up for their rights. "You're as good as anybody else, don't care what their color is." But as soon as he had put her teachings into practice, she had let him down. He was coming home from school almost four months ago (time sure did haul ass) and came upon some white boys messing with his sister, had her down on the ground, and their hands underneath her dress, and he jumped in to protect her, beat the hell outa them peckerwoods, and the policeman came up and arrested him and sent Jenny Lee for his mother to come to the courthouse, and

Mama beat him in a courthouse room in front of two cracker policemen for fighting for his sister! (He would never forgive her!) *The long tall cracker cop said, "Whup that boy, Laurie—You don't want us to put him in the reformatory, do you? After all, he was fighting white boys."*

And Mama pleading with the two cracker cops like she had no shame at all and the crackers' faces getting redder and meaner and "Whup that boy—You better whup that boy. He's gittin off light. Reformatory's fulla boys like him—" And finally Mama whipping him on his naked back till the natural blood came.

He could feel the whip now biting into his back like an angry rattlesnake. And he would never be close to Mama again. Sometimes he wanted to break the wall between them, him and Mama, wanted things to be like they used to be, and he knew that Mama wanted it too. Sometimes he understood what had made Mama do it—the reformatory and what it had done to her brother, Tim, many years ago when Mama was a girl. She had explained it to him a hundred times. But he never could accept her explanation. How could he!

> AIN'T GONE COUNT BUT ONE MORE TIME
> HONEY IN THE BEE FA
> I CAN'T SEE YA
> ALL HIDDEE————?

"Come on, get up off your fat ass and play."

> ALL IN THE DITCH IS CAUGHT—

Robby looked around and up into Fat Gus's face. "Aw I don't feel like it."

Gus raised his bushy eyebrows and gestured with his wide signifying eyes and swayed his tubby body from side to side and nodded his big round head in the direction of Ida Mae. "What you feel like doing?"

A strange warmth flowed into Robby's face, a sweet and guilty feeling. "I don't feel like playing no TEN TEN DOUBLE TEN. That's a game for little biddy children anyhow."

> ALL AROUND MY BASE IS CAUGHT.

"Ida Mae like to play TEN TEN DOUBLE TEN," Gus said, nodding towards Ida Mae with a devilish look in his wide open face. "What you feel like doing?" He was Robby's best buddy but he had an effortless way of getting on Robby's nerves.

Robby's neck collected an angry sweaty heat. "I don't feel like fooling around today, Gus. Don't mess with me."

Gus changed his tactics. "How's Miss Laurie Lee?" he asked Robby softly, sweetly, tenderly.

Robby stood up, his narrow eyes narrowing almost shut. "Leave my mother out of it. I don't allow anybody to talk about my mother. You know me better'n that."

Gus's devilish face looked so innocent, he might have been an angel paying a short sweet visit down here on earth. "Ain' nobody talking about Miss Laurie Lee. She's the sweetest lady that ever lived on God's green—"

Robby said, "I told you, Gus—Keep my Mama's name outa your mouth. I don't play no dozens never!"

Gus said, "What's the matter with you? All I said was Miss Laurie Lee—"

He didn't get any further because Robby went upside his head with both fists and swarmed all over Gus with the tears streaming down Robby's face, and down to the ground he and his best buddy went and rolling over and over and puffing and blowing, and the game broke up and the children made a dusty circle around Robby and Gus—and—

"Get him, Robby! Make him say Sweet Papa!"

"Atta Boy, Gus! You got the business!"

Through all the laughing and the yelling Robby heard Ida Mae's sweet welcomed voice. "Y'all ought to be shame of yourselves! I just declare!" And Robby *was* ashamed, but shame didn't have anything to do with it. Ida Mae Raglin and a great big boy named Jake Billy pulled the two best buddies apart. They were on their feet now puffing and blowing and both of them crying and their nostrils running and Ida Mae holding Robby and Jake Billy holding Gus. Both of them, their manhood smelling like peanuts roasting on an open fire, looking sweaty and grim and mean and angry and anxious to continue the thing they had started.

A boy named Jimmy yelled, "Let 'em fight, they ain't no kin."

Another boy shouted, "One sked and the other'n glad of it."

Another one yelled, "Turn me loose—you better hold me, Jake!"

The children whooped and hollered.

Gus made a half-hearted attempt to pull away from Jake Billy and Robby said, "Turn him loose, don't hold him!" But the fight was over and everybody knew it. And Robby was aware of Ida Mae's arms around him and her body against his sweaty body and the smells of her young and womanish body mixed with his own like fresh coffee cooking. He didn't care if she never turned him loose.

Jake Billy said, "I ought to make you two sap-suckers kiss and make up." And everybody laughed and giggled. Ida Mae gave Robby her handkerchief and he wiped his face and put his shirt back inside of his trousers, as the other children ran off yelling to watch two dogs who were desperately stuck together and yelping and running around in circles. Robby looked slyly at Ida Mae as she stared at the newly-sprouted grass with a shame-faced look that made her round cheeks look like fallen apples sweetly kissed by the noon-day sun. And she was his girl with her large wide eyes and roundish mouth and her plump legs covered by black cotton stockings that reached above her knees, and a brief flash of cinnamon-colored thighs between her stockings and her gingham dress and her body not as shapeless as it used to be but still a little awkward as it reached desperately toward womanhood. He looked past her at the poor dogs yelping and running around and pulling each other back and forth like a tug of war, and the children jumping up and down and kicking up dust, and making more noise than the dogs were making. His face grew even warmer, as he remembered the first time he had seen two dogs stuck together in front of Old Lady Sarah's house which was next to his. He had run into his house to Mama and cried out to her that Old Lady Sarah had tied two dogs together and would Mama go out and untie them, they were suffering something awful. And Mama had turned her head and smiled on the sly, but she had gone outside with a dishpan full of water and had thrown it on the dogs. The kids yelled louder and louder and he looked slyly at his sweetheart and wished he had a pan of water.

"Let's go," he said like he was angry with his girlfriend.

They walked a short distance to her house in silence. Most of the time he walked with his eyes straight ahead of him, every now and then stealing glances at her pretty face in profile. The air was filled with pine scents as the dying day gave up the ghost. When they reached her house he stood with her at the gate in front of the house. He looked at her and through her like he was dreaming in the daytime, staring at the shining new greenness everywhere all over the yard and near the front porch and the gleaming bed of yellow roses. He swallowed hard.

"Spring sure did come quick and it sure is pretty." A soft breeze blowing past his ears like the rustle of a squirrel moving swiftly through dry autumn leaves. And Ida Mae's bosom beginning to swell up and puff out slightly like a full grown woman's bosom. And spring was the prettiest time of the year to Rob, until summertime arrived.

She stared at him. "You can say that again."

His stomach tumbled head over heels. His nostrils crinkled with the heavy smell of greenness mixed up with the softer smell of yellow roses and honeysuckles climbing up the side of the porch.

She said, "You ought to be shame of yourself though—you and Fat Gus—fighting over me like mannish puppies."

His face broke out with a brand new perspiration. "Wasn't nobody fighting over you."

She said knowingly, "Boys ain't got a bit of sense. Fighting over a girl ain't going to make a girl like you, if she don't already like you."

"It didn't have nothing to do with you."

She said, "What was it about then?"

He said, "You must think you a piece of gold or something. Fighting over you—Humph—I bet that's something." He couldn't tell her he had hit Gus because he'd asked him how his mother was. She would think he was a fool or something. Fighting your best buddy because he asked about your mother's health. A girl would never understand it.

She said, "What was it about then?" She was angry. He could tell by the beads of sweat above her lips and on her nose and the fire building in her eyes and her hand upon her slender hips. And the bumblebees that buzzed like crazy in *his* stomach.

He didn't even want the word mother in his mouth now, and even so how could he tell her or anybody else about his mother? How could he explain to anybody how much he loved her and at the same time hated her more than anything else in the world? How could he explain it to somebody else when he could not explain it to himself. Yet Ida Mae was his girlfriend, and the last thing he wanted to do was to make his sweetheart angry. He wanted to tell her he loved her and he knew that she loved him, and to hell with big old fathead Fat Gus, and all the little Fat Gusses, wherever they were.

She said, "What's the matter with you? The cat got your tongue or something? I asked you, what were you fighting about then?"

He said, "You don't look like my Mama to me and you sure couldn't be my Daddy. Tend to your business and leave mine alone."

And she stared at him and he wanted to take her in his arms and hug and kiss his sweetheart with her warm eyes growing wider, larger, and filling up with hurt and her thick and roundish lips a-trembling.

She said, "I hate that about you, Rob Youngblood! I declare I do!" And she turned and walked away from him down the path to her front porch, and he stood there watching his sweetheart go, and he was all alone in the world now, and he blamed his mother, and he hated his mother, he hated her more than ever before.

He had lost his best buddy and his best girl in one afternoon and it was all his mother's fault. Might as well go home. There was nowhere else to go. It was almost dark and Daddy would be home by now. Daddy was a great big tall man strong as a mule and he could wrestle with a horse. And Daddy wouldn't take any shit off crackers. That was one sure thing. Last Saturday afternoon Daddy and Robby played catch over in the vacant lot, and coming home afterwards Daddy put his heavy arm around Robby's shoulders. His voice like the soft rumble of thunder on a summer afternoon.

"Your mother, Rob, they don't make em no better—the wonderfullest woman on God's green earth." Well one sure thing, Rob and his Daddy didn't take any stuff off of any peckerwood riding or walking sitting down or talking. He tried to spit through his teeth like Fat Gus did, and he picked up a rock and threw it at an old tin can in the middle of the road. The can jumped in the air like a dog gone crazy with heat. He smiled, and continued up the dusty road. There were no sidewalks in his part of town. And no pavement.

He was in front of his house now but he did not want to go inside. The one-story two-room house sat quietly amongst the shadows of the dying day and high off the ground and back from the red-clay street. He walked slowly up the clumsy steps and opened the door. Mama was sitting at the old-fashioned sewing machine. The humming stopped as she looked around at her angry boy.

"Well, how're you, Mr. Man? What's on the rail for the lizard?" she asked in a teasing tone, her eyes deliberately widening for him. Her deep dark narrow eyes that understood everything in the whole wide world.

"I'm all right, Mama," he mumbled, not looking in her direction, not even seeing her arms stretched out toward him, and yet he sensed that she wanted him to come to her, to be embraced by her, making everything all right like she used to do. Yet, now, at this moment, he remembered the courthouse whipping, could feel the whip bite into his back and the blood begin to flow. He wanted to be mean to her, made himself keep his face turned from her. A slap in her face that she deserved.

She looked back at him, saw his angry jaws moving up and down, working on an old stick of chewing gum he had found in his pocket. "You come in this house," she said, "eating something good, didn't offer your poor old mother a taste. Didn't even say—old doggie, here's a bone."

He mumbled under his breath as he started towards the kitchen. "If the Lord keep the smell out of your nose, I'll sure keep the taste out your mouth."

She smiled at his back. "Big Sister waited for you a good while, son. Went out to Anty's to get some of that good old clabber milk."

The boy looked back at her for a moment and answered her with an angry frown. "Got to get my stuff in for tonight," he finally mumbled, leaving his mother with the smile on her face that dammit he still loved. There was so much between them that brought them together and at the same time kept them apart. They were so much alike—he and his mother—the high forehead, the dark narrow eyes, the mouth going around continuous curves. Their skin possessed the same deep variation of black and tan and brownish-black blending and clashing, and at eleven years old he was as big as his mother, a little taller even. And she was really the one he loved and respected above all others. Excepting Daddy—maybe. He walked heavily through the kitchen to the backyard to chop up some kindling and bring in wood for the cooking stove.

When he finished his chores, he sat at the kitchen table, smelling the sharp rusty heat from the stove, an old newspaper before his eyes, reading absolutely nothing. The hum from the sewing machine stopped. He waited. His mother's work was never done. Her voice from the other room said, "You finished with the kindling and the wood, son?"

"Yes'm." She knew he had finished. She didn't have to make her voice sound so damn sweet to him either. Let her leave him alone!

"Come here a minute. I want you to go over to Hawkins' and get a loaf of light bread for supper. Sliced bread—Sanders' sliced bread."

"Yes'm."

He came into the room, stood before her straight as a telegraph post, and slim as a pine sapling, like a soldier except for his pigeon toes. He was built like his Daddy and pigeon-toed just like Joe Youngblood, and powerfully constructed. Mama had a face that was never harsh. Of late she seemed to live in tender shadows and soft reflective meditations. And yet when Mama smiled it was like the sudden glow of daybreak.

He turned his head from her in anguish. She gave him the money. "Now don't stop at Spivey's," she said. "He doesn't carry sliced bread."

He breathed a deep and angry sigh. "I know, Mama."

It was getting dark now, and as he walked along the dusty street, he wondered where his Daddy was. His Daddy—His Daddy—His Daddy! In Hawkins' Grocery Store his nose picked up the color of damp sawdust sprinkled on the cement floor. Sharp and moldish like the smell of fallen leaves, autumn brown, wet and heavy with a brand new rain. He liked the odor of damp sawdust, but a frown settled over his face as he waited around to be served. His eyes took in the counter where the bread was, focused themselves on the delicious-looking cinnamon buns, heavily coated with melt-in-the mouth icing and punctured here and there with juicy raisins, but he had been sent for Sanders' Sliced Bread. And Mr. Hawkins wasn't the meanest cracker in Cross County, Georgia.

It was Robby's turn now to be waited on, but the red-headed, fat-like-a-barrel grocer looked past him and spoke to a white man who had just walked into the store. "What's it going to be today, Mr. Coleman?"

And Mr. Coleman with his short, squatty, crackerish self walked right up and gave his order as if it were commonly understood that Robby Youngblood had all the time in the world. Robby's entire body flamed with anger. But Mr. Hawkins was a pink-faced white man and the only one that sold Sanders' Bread, already sliced. And he really didn't mean any harm at all. Robby could go all the way to the Big Store, but that would take too long, and Mama was waiting. As the anger mounted inside of him, his tongue slipped noiselessly over his lips and he tasted his great anger. Mr. Hawkins and Mr. Coleman and the plainclothesman and Sheriff Skinny McGuire down at the courthouse were all together one big white evil wall reaching from Heaven deep down into Hell, and likewise the white woman that came in and was waited on before Robby and the little boy with the note his mother had sent and white white white was mean and ugly and white was the color that stood for evil. And also the peckerwood kids that jumped on Big Sister were mixed up with Mr. Hawkins and Sheriff McGuire and the big white wall, as were the white school boys who Robby and his used-to-be buddy, Gus, had rock-battled a couple of weeks ago, saying nothing to Mama about it.

Finally the pleasant-faced Mr. Hawkins took notice of the arrogant-looking Youngblood boy.—"What fer yer, Youngblood?"

"Nothing fer yer—yer peckerwood sonofabitch." Robby Youngblood mumbled. But, mad as he was with this white man, he was twice as angry with Mama for sending him into such a trap. It was Mama's fault! It was all her fault.

"Take the shit out of your mouth, boy," the grocer kidded. "You want something on credit this evening, don't be shame about it."

"Loaf of Sanders' Sliced Bread, and I got my money to pay for it."

In the same kindly playful frame of mind the tall fat white man took up the loaf of bread and, holding it like a football, threw it to Robby. "We wanna touchdown!" But Robby deliberately stepped out of the way of the forward pass and the bread went through the screen door left open by the little white boy and ended up on the unpaved sidewalk, kicking up a little evening dust.

The white man's face flushed red and unpleasant. "All right, boy, give me the money."

"All right, man, give me the bread."

"It's out there on the sidewalk, boy. I threw it to you. Sho-shoulda caught—" The man was so angry his tongue began to twist and the words to stumble over each other as they tumbled out of his mouth.

"You don't throw things at me when I come in this store," Robby said. "When I order something, you wrap it up or put it in a bag and hand it to me over the counter. What do you take me for? This ain't no football field. This supposed to be a grocery store."

The man started from behind the counter. "Why you sassy little dirty black bastard!"

Robby's hand reached out quickly and he picked up an overripe tomato out of a vegetable bin and at that moment all of his hatred for the things that made Mama whip him in Mr. Cross's Courthouse came together in Mr. Hawkin's face which to Robby was white and as hideous as a ghost in a nightmare and mean and evil and quickly he drew his arm back and hurled the tomato in all his great anger at Mr. Hawkins and the policemen in the Courthouse and the white boys who molested his sister and even Mama who wore a white mask now, and it landed in Mr. Hawkins' red puffy face, juice spattering everywhere. He turned and dashed out of Hawkins' store and around the corner and up Planters Street.

Mr. Hawkins ran out of the store after him. "Come back here, little nigger!"

Robby was scared and a fierce hatred filled up his face and his body, but there was a certain pleasant feeling flowing through the muscles of his powerful young legs, as he ran and ran and ran and ran.

When he was sure the fat white man wasn't chasing him anymore, he slowed down gradually, his breathing and heartbeat coming short and quick-like. His body was covered with a shivering sweat, soaking his head and his neck and his back and draining from his armpits. He stopped at Spivey's for a loaf of bread—not sliced.

By the time he reached home he had gotten himself together. He had wiped the sweat from his face and neck with his shirttail. He walked through the house and put the bread on the kitchen table. Big Sister was setting the table for supper.

"Hi, Big Stuff." That's what he called her sometimes when he felt especially big himself, and, as frightened as he was, he felt pretty big to-night, because he had challenged the goddamn white man. He was a Youngblood—Joe Youngblood's boy—the Youngbloods was one bunch of Black folks that didn't take any stuff off of white folks.

"Hi," she said—then added, "My name ain't no Big Stuff."

He made a funny face at his sister and poked out his tongue.

Mama turned from the stove, looked at her children and at the loaf of bread Rob had put on the table. She knew instantly that the bread wasn't Sanders' sliced, but she didn't want to say anything, didn't want to start anything that would inevitably result in an argument between her and her baby. Here of late every little thing got out of control and turned quickly into an angry argument. She turned back to the stove, turned the liver over in the spider, listening to the hissing sound that it made, and she knew without looking that his mouth would be watering, because he really loved cow liver and good old liver gravy. So drop the question of Sanders' Sliced Bread—what difference does it make anyhow. She didn't want to, but she felt the words forming in her mouth and she heard herself asking him—"How come you didn't get Sanders' Sliced Bread, son?"

"Didn't have any," he said, standing at the other end of the table with his back to his mother.

"Hawkins always carries sliced bread," Laurie told him, walking away from the hot stove. Bread was bread—what difference did it make, she told herself in helpless anger.

"Didn't get it from Hawkins!" he almost shouted. Now he looked at her, open-faced and sassy. God! How things had changed between them —Would it go on like this forever and ever? She loved her baby—She loved her baby!

"But I particularly told you to get that new Sanders' Sliced Bread. I particularly told you to go to Hawkins."

"I did go to Hawkins."

"Don't get mixed up, son. What happened you didn't get the sliced bread like I told you?"

"You gonna whip me, Mama?" He was whipping her, coldly and deliberately. He was whipping her on her naked soul.

"Never you mind about that. You just tell me what happened—about the bread."

He looked around the kitchen. "Where's Daddy? How come he didn't come home yet?"

Big Sister said, "Daddy had to go by Brother Williams to pay his lodge dues."

"Robby, you hear me talking to you?" Mama said. Her patience giving out.

"You aren't going to whip me, are you?"

Laurie's shoulders sagged, a deep sigh slipped noisily from her lips. What was this whipping to do? Anybody'd think she did nothing but whip her children for breakfast, dinner and supper. "Never you mind the whipping. What about the bread? Tell me the truth."

She looked at her boy. He had left her now—thinking away into time and space, remembering another day—maybe. Why should he trust her? Then he looked her full in the face again. Why should he trust her? "I went to Hawkins, but he was out of Sanders' Bread. That's how come I went to the other store—Mr. Spivey's."

But she knew he was lying, deliberately lying, and she felt like shaking the truth out of him and beating the sassy look from his face. "Why didn't you say so in the first place?"

"I was trying to tell you but you wouldn't let me." He looked down at the floor and then defiantly up into her eyes again. Standing for a moment looking blankly through her and past her, his narrow eyes opened wide. Hate and anger in his face as clean and naked as sunlight on a windowpane. "I've got to go to the toilet," he announced. He opened the back door and was gone before she could think of anything to say.

She turned and walked back towards the stove. She was shaking and her brow was damp and suddenly her head began to ache and throb now like a rotten tooth. Laurie tried to take hold of herself. Why make all this big to do about a loaf of light bread? She felt the girl watching her, eyes growing wider and batting nervously, taking sides with the boy. She went to the stove, took the meat out of the spider and made the gravy.

"You finished setting the table, daughter?"

"Yes'm." Agitation in the girl's voice.

The boy had not come back into the house. Laurie went into the next room and made a charcoal fire in the fireplace. She had ironing to do after supper. God—Jehovah! She worked all day and half the night— And for what? In her own house she didn't even have peace with her children at the end of the day. She went back into the kitchen and was busying herself about the stove, waiting for the boy to come back into the house, when BANG—BANG—BANG! As if somebody were trying to break the front door down. What in the name of God? As she opened the door a big fat tub-belly white man moved past her into the front room. He wore a gray hat and a white apron reached below his coat. He looked around the room as if he had lost something.

Laurie knew instantly that white folks were after her boy again, and she felt sick and cold and her knees got weak. She was sinking sinking in deep white marshy water and her head began to swim.

"Where's that boy? Where's that boy?" Great big angry white man—his dark nervous eyes, his juicy lips, everything about him was contemptuous and angry.

"What boy, Mr. Hawkins?" She tried to keep the fear from her face and the trembling out of her voice.

"You—you—you know what boy—your boy—Rob—or Robby or whatever you call him—"

"What's the matter, Mr. Hawkins?" Her face was filling up and a fullness in her shoulders and her stomach somersaulting. "He didn't mean any harm, Mr. Hawkins."

"They don't never mean no harm. Did he tell you what happened in my store while ago?"

"No, sir, Mr. Hawkins, I can't rightly say he did." She turned to Jenny Lee who stood wide-legged in the doorway to the kitchen. "Go get Robby, Big Sister. Tell him I say come here right away."

Big Sister said, "Yes mam."

The white man waited impatiently, his hat still perched on top of a red mess of rumpled hair. Laurie busied herself at the fireplace, appearing not to notice Hawkins. Big Sister came back into the room.

"He's still in the toilet," Big Sister told Mama with rebellion in her own voice, her big eyes wide and sassy.

"Well tell him to come in here right away and no messing around."

That's just what he is doing—messing, Jenny Lee was tempted to say, as she stood facing her mother, her mouth poking out and her thin shoulders thrust forward, her big wide brown eyes narrowing in anger now.

"Gone now, girl. Tell him I don't want to have to come out there and get him my own self."

"Yes'm—Mama—" Jenny Lee said fiercely.

"Yeah," Mr. Hawkins said. "Cause I'm in a hurry. Doggonnit, I got a business to run. I had to lock up my store!"

Mr. Hawkins put his weight on one foot, then on the other. He coughed and cleared his throat and readjusted the hat on his head. A gray smoke issued from the fireplace. Laurie's eyes ran water as she adjusted the charcoals with the poke. She wiped the bottom of the irons and she placed them on the coals. She tried desperately to keep her hands from trembling.

Big Sister came back, the boy dragging behind her. Hawkins came suddenly back to life. "There he is—Ask him what he done in my store. Go ahead, woman, ask him!"

There was a tiredness in Laurie's voice now, an emptiness that wasn't really emptiness in her eyes. Something that said—Leave us alone— Leave us alone! "What's it all about, son?"

The boy hesitated, a terrible fear in his eyes that she did not want to see. He looked from one to the other of the grown folks, and then his eyes came to rest on Big Sister as if she were his only friend. "I didn't do nothing."

The great big fat man jumped towards the boy. "Yes you did! Yes you did! And you gonna say so right now!"

"Now wait a minute, Mr. Hawkins," Laurie said quietly. "Please now —Let me handle it."

"All right—All right—but you better make him tell the truth!"

"Come on now, Robby," her weary voice said. "Speak up. Tell me the truth, son."

The boy's head sank beneath his shoulders, his eyes staring at the floor and he didn't say a mumbling word.

"Robby! What did you do? What happened?"

The boy's frightened eyes stared harder and harder at the bare scrubbed-colorless floor. The calm left Laurie Lee's face now. She shook him by the shoulders. "You hear me talking to you, Robby? What happened—what happened?"

He became more frightened. It was terrible for her to see the awful fear in her baby's eyes. Jenny Lee came over and took him by the hand. "Don't let this old fat-head peckerwood scare you, Robby," she said. He looked at his sister and his eyes widened, then almost closed completely, mashing out a single tear which fell down his face onto his curvy mouth. Both of them standing there close to their mother but far far away. Timid and cautious like two dogs tentatively sniffing the smell of a human stranger and sharply alerted for a sudden kick-in-the-face. They were poised for flight. She was their mother, she was no stranger, she was their mother. She felt like beating the innocence from their faces. Didn't they know she was their mother?

"I'll tell you what he done. Come into my store this evening and I gave him a loaf of light bread, but he wouldn't take it. He threw one of my tomatoes at me. Hit me in the face!"

She knew they were afraid she would betray them to the white man, and the knowledge made her angry, but she knew now what she had to do. There was no other course to take. Her stomach quivered and her body broke into a sweat.

"There must have been a reason, Mr. Hawkins. My boy wouldn't do that, just so."

"What you mean a reason? Ain' no reason for a nigger boy to act that way to white folks."

She looked at the cracker. *Aah—Lord, Joe Youngblood should be here. You wouldn't talk so biggedy then, Mr. White Man.* And yet she was glad that Joe wasn't there. He would get into enough trouble in a half a minute to last him a whole lifetime. "What did you do to him first?" she asked the peckerwood.

The cracker's fat stomach went in and out, his face flushing redder than it already was. He breathed hard and loud like an asthma victim. "Nothing, woman, I done told you. He musta got the devil in him."

Laurie turned to Robby. "There must've been a reason," she said. "What about it, son?"

"You mean to stand up there, woman, and call me a liar?"

His mother asked him, "What about it, Robby?"

"Tell her, Robby. Don't be scared."

He pulled his hand away from Big Sister's. His fists balled up. At that moment his mother's face had become the powerful beautiful image he had almost forgotten. His mother, a little more than five feet of powerful woman cast in bronze, with a strong and lovely visage. For him, there was foreverness in her face like a mighty river that goes on and on and always was and always will be. "It wasn't like what he said, Mama. It wasn't like that at all." She had always been his Rock of Ages. His head was up now—where it belonged—staring his mother in the face. Hawkins might not have been in the room at all.

"Tell me, son."

"I went to the store like you told me, Mama. Had to stand around for a long time for him to wait on white folks that came in the store after I did. Made me mad. So after there wasn't any more white folks in the store, he says to me—what fer yer?—like that. So I said—a loaf of Sanders' Sliced Bread like you told me. So he took it up and threw it to me. I stepped out of the—"

"Woman, are you gonna stand there and listen to that sassy boy?"

"He called me a bad name too."

"What did he call you, son?"

"Well I be goddamn—" From the white gentleman.

"He called me, Mama—He called me—"

"Never mind, son. I got a good idea what it was. Don't dirty your mouth."

Hawkin's face was fire and blood and red-hot brimstone, his big lips moving before the words formed. The blood pounding through his forehead like a stroke of apoplexy. "Wo—Woman, are—are you gonna whup that boy right here in front of me or ain't you?"

"Do what?"

"You ain't deef, woman. Whup him right here in front of me—that's what!"

She could see Robby's face drawn tight and determined. His eyes narrowed and rebellious, fright replaced by hope and confidence. Jenny Lee with her lips pressed together, bottom one sticking out and her tiny fists balled up. Did they think she would let them down? Her brother, Tim, came back to her like a resurrected nightmare long forgotten. The ugly gray building of Cross County Reformatory seemed to descend upon her and her children and close in on them. She struggled hard to keep her entire body from trembling. Great God Almighty give her strength! She didn't want any trouble with white folks, but they gave her very little choice. Maybe if she told him she would whip Robby later on this evening after she was rested. Maybe he would go back to his store and leave everything to her.

She turned to the angry white man. "Mr. Hawkins, please—" The hateful words stuck in her throat, as bitter now as chicken bile.

Mr. Hawkins said, "Woman, is you or ain't you?"

She could feel Joe Youngblood in the house. Lord give her strength, Dear Jesus! Ever since that day in the courthouse—Was it a long time ago?—even way before, everything had been geared towards this moment. White folks had destroyed her brother's life, kicked her son around. Tried every way to break her husband's spirit. Had nearly worked her to death, molested her daughter, divided her family and then turned her children against her. She fumbled around now in the darkness of her mind's great desperation. Searching for the words that would melt this white man's frozen heart. Surely there were words somewhere to rescue her. She thought she might say, "Please, Mister Hawkins, we always been good, polite, law-abiding, hard-working colored people—" Instead, she heard herself say, "Why should I whup him?"

"Why should you?" the white man blustered. "Why—Why should you?"—Why—why—to teach him his place—teach him better'n—"

The Reformatory, Laurie, the Reformatory—Remember Tim—Remember Tim—lost and gone these many years—

"He hasn't got any place but to stand up for his rights. You white folks picked on us one time too many—"

"Why you sassy, black nigger bitch!"

She looked at the big-fat-belly white gentleman with the red mess of hair and the gray hat still on his head. Looked him up and down, her eyes brimming with contempt, a rejoiced-in, heart-felt contempt, for everything he represented.

"Tell me," she asked, like she was asking somebody to tell her the time of day, "how in the hell can two hard grown folks sassy one another?"

She stood wide-legged and firm. Her eyes, her whole being said she was ready for anything.

The children—the children—she felt the strength of the children united inside of her, giving her even greater strength. And GreatGodAl-mighty—Joe Youngblood! She looked up into the eyes of the cracker and she knew a merging inside of her of the children's strength and Joe Youngblood's and her mother and her mother's mother and her father. She took the white rag and picked up a red hot iron and put it on a pad on the ironing board within her reach. Fighting back was the only language they understood. The white gentleman finally took his hat off in the lady's presence and threw it to the floor. "You one nigger whore I'm gonna teach a lesson this evening."

Her face was covered with an angry sweat. Perspiration crawled over her back from shoulder to shoulder like an army on the march. "Man I'd be happy to do time on the chain gang for an old white peckerwood like you." Her fingers in the white piece of cloth wrapped themselves around the handle of the smoking iron.

The gentleman started towards her. The children got between him and their mother, making angry balls out of their fists. They had never heard her swear before—the children—but it sounded good to them this time.

"Get out of my house goddammit!" She stood her ground with the red hot iron in her hand now. Big Sister grabbed the poker. Robby moved in to meet the cracker with his powerful fists.

Hawkins pulled up short and stared at them. "You ain't heard the last of this, old nigger woman!" he said as he turned and walked towards the door and out of the house. "Goddamn sassy nigger bitch!"

Laurie Lee stood there for a moment, her hand encircling the handle of the iron. She put the iron on the board and wiped the sweat from her face with the hot rag and more sweat came. Robby picked up old man Hawkins' hat and threw it in the open fire. And the boy went to his mother. Big Sister dropped the poker and went and put her arms around her mother. Laurie Lee fought back the tears that stood on the other side of her eyes, and she shook all over. She was the children's mother. And they knew she was their mother. And Joe Youngblood was their father.

The white man's hat burning in the fireplace threw a gray-white smoke into the room.

ESSAYS

"She'll Speak to Generations Yet To Come"

I am indeed happy to see the development of a tribute such as this in honor of the distinguished African American writer Miss Gwendolyn Brooks. I have had a long association with this fine poet which began long before recognition and fame which she well deserved came to her. I am reminded that she and I have shared some mighty precious moments and passed several important milestones. Yes, back in the thirties, we marched in Anti-Lynching parades up and down the Southside as members of the NAACP Youth Council. Whether the youth of today recognize it or not, that was the most militant organization for young people going outside of the Left. We studied and wrote poetry in a class at the South Side Community Art Center taught by Inez Cunningham Stark, yes, a fine white woman and patron to many creative people regardless of color. A contest was held in which naturally Gwendolyn won first prize. We were not surprised. We knew she was good and gifted way back then. We were not the least bit surprised when later, our city, the state and the nation finally caught up with what we knew all the time. We wondered what took them so long in honoring and according this poet the place which she deserved. Gwendolyn and I were college students; then engaged; then married; we shared the joy of looking upon our first borns, her Henry Jr. and my Gayle, born I believe in the same year. We shared the heartbreak at the passing of loved ones. And now I share with all of you this salute to Gwendolyn tendered by members of the black and white community.

Yes, at long last, some segments of the black community have arrived at the point of treasuring, expressing appreciation for and erecting lasting monuments to their artists. It has been a long time coming but thank Goodness it has come at last! Better late than never.

Today many people are saluting the moment and black is beautiful and accolades and awards are heaped upon the poet. But whether she received these things or not Miss Brooks's works will be remembered. Miss Brooks will be remembered.

Will she be remembered because of a limited vocabulary filled with sensational and titillating four letter words used and excused on the basis of relevancy? I think not.

Will she be remembered because her poetry is filled with rage, hate and violence, that hate which is the antithesis of creativity, that hate which corrupts, destroys, and thwarts creativity? I think not.

Will she be remembered because she has mastered the dexterity to embroider cute designs on the page with a typewriter? I think not.

Miss Brooks and her poetry will be remembered and will speak to generations yet to come because in the first instance she is a creative human being who is concerned with all humanity. She will be remembered because she speaks from the deep wellsprings of her own black experience which shares common universals with all downtrodden and oppressed peoples, black, brown, red, white and yellow.

However above all, there is this fact which should be of great import to all younger poets who would seek to emulate Miss Brooks; Miss Brooks is a student and scholar of poetry and writing. She has done and continues to do her homework, that meticulous dedication which is necessary to produce a meaningful and lasting work of art. Miss Brooks has thoroughly mastered her craft. She knows it inside and out and in all of its aspects. She does not resort to fads, tricks or gimmicks of the moment.

This to me, is the important lesson to be gained from reflecting on, saluting and honoring my long time friend Gwendolyn Brooks. But the best way to salute or honor this black writer or any black writer is to buy her books. In a quiet moment, take up a volume of Brooks poetry or prose. Read it. Study it. Perhaps you will find out why it is considered a contribution to American culture and to world culture. This will be a rewarding experience for you as it has been, is being for countless thousands of others.

December 31, 1969

"Home Has Always Been Blackness"
For Sister Gwen Brooks

You can rest now, Sister Gwen! The point's been made. You're home now and you no longer have to worry about those meaningless, cruel little critics who thought you were captured by somebody else. The white folks maybe. Or maybe the middle-class negroes. School teachers, doctors, lawyers, architects, businessmen, "civic leaders"?

No, Gwen, you were never their captive, nor their spokesman; a friend to a few, perhaps, a peripheral acquaintance to some, but never "their" poetess.

You knew some of them, but more fundamentally you knew and wrote about black people. You knew a lot of them too! Like Oscar Brown, and Frank London Brown, and Langston Hughes; the 47th St. 'L'; 63rd and Cottage. Remember the Mecca?

Who has known and loved black people of Chicago more than you, Gwen baby? Nobody! But some of the critics kept on sniping and digging where there was only dirt to find, never looking for the truth and beauty and dignity which were within you all the time.

Now comes your discovery of blackness—a richness, goodness and depth of humanity never known before. And you embrace it—and it embraces you. There's an instant love affair! But it's only a renewal of your old self with a newer, more energetic, enlightened and determined generation of black people.

It's black people who have changed, Gwen, not you. You have only regenerated. You did what we knew you would do because we knew where you were all the time.

When you began teaching writing classes to young black gang members—you were consistent with your old self. You were the same Gwen Brooks who won the Pulitzer in 1950, with a new dimension and sense of mission.

When you started inviting young black writers to your home—giving them the greatest encouragement, inspiration and intellectual stimulation of their lives—you were consistent.

When you helped some of these same writers to travel and gain greater exposure—indispensable to any writer who takes life and his art seriously—you were consistent, Sister Gwen.

When you rejected, sometimes subtly, sometimes out of hand, the old, pallid patronizing friendships of unsympathetic and indifferent whites, you were consistent.

Your whole life has been consistent, Gwen, very much predictable if one knows your humble beginnings, and the simple, dedicated life you have led, even after winning one of the highest literary honors white America had to bestow.

Neither the Pulitzer Prize, the resulting smiles of misplaced affection and hypocrisy, nor the poet laureate's honor from the state of Illinois changed you, Gwen. You remained constant—simple, humble, devoted to your art and to black people.

The point need not be stressed that an affirmation of your blackness was, according to white America's narrow definition of "universality," a testimony to your belief in the goodness and beauty of mankind.

In sum, Gwen, it's your critics and not you who need to look at where they are. They are the inconstant ones, not you.

And now, come some new detractors, mostly white, some negro, who, with feigned sadness and concealed outrage, say that you have betrayed "universal" poetic forms and become the captive of some "negative, anti-white, parochial black militants."

Pity and sorrow on these poor people. Or, better, forget them! For their irrelevance requires hardly a passing glance, much less a serious analysis or rebuttal.

Forget them! For they know neither Gwen Brooks, the black people she loves so much, nor the new forces which are shaping their lives—and America's destiny.

There is much work to be done—much more unity to forge—much more building to do. The world we give to the next generation must be freer and more humane than the one we knew. That's why we don't have a minute—not a second—to waste on trivia and irrelevancies. The creation of a new humanity has been your work ever since this land was blessed with your genius, Gwen. That's why you're home, Gwen, in your natural place of work, comfort, renewal and final rest.

Home is where your action is, Gwen. It's been love to share it with you.

An Afterword: for gwen
(the search for the new-song begins with the old)

knowing her is not knowing her.
is not
autograph lines or souvenir signatures & shared smiles,
is not
pulitzers, poet laureates or honorary degrees,
you see   we ordinary people
just know
ordinary people.

to read gwen is to be,
to experience her in the *real*
is the same, she is her words.   more
like a fixed part of the world   is there
quietly penetrating   slow
reminds us of a willie kgositsile love poem   or
isaac hayes singing "one woman."

still
she suggests more;
have u ever seen her home?
it's an idea of her: a brown wooden frame
trimmed in dark gray with a new screen door.
inside: looks like the lady owes everybody on the southside
              nothing but books momma's books.
her home like her person is under-fed and small.

gwen:
pours smiles of african-rain
a pleasure well received among uncollected garbage cans
and heatless basement apartments.
her voice the needle for new-songs
plays unsolicited messages: poets, we've all seen
poets. minor poets ruined by
minor fame.

BIOGRAPHICAL NOTES

Biographical Notes

ahmed akinwole alhamisi—spiritual poet. applied artist. aquarian vegetarian.

Samuel Allen—has been poet-in-residence at Tuskegee Institute and is presently in residence at Wesleyan University in Connecticut. A graduate of Fisk University with an LL.B. from Harvard Law School, he has published numerous articles and essays on the African and Caribbean poets of *negritude*. A volume of his poetry, *Ivory Tusks,* was published in a bilingual edition in Germany in 1956 under the pen name "Paul Vesey."

johari amini (Jewel C. Latimore)—a Chicago poet, has published three volumes of poetry, *Images in Black, Black Essence* and *Let's Go Somewhere.* She is Kuumba writer-in-residence and a member of the Organization of Black American Culture (OBAC) Writers' Workshop and of the Gwendolyn Brooks Writers' Workshop.

Lerone Bennett Jr.—one of the leading black intellectuals of our time and a prolific writer and lecturer, is senior editor of *Ebony*. He served, in 1969, as Senior Fellow at the Institute of the Black World in Atlanta. His six works of Afro-American history have won him an international reputation as a scholar and historian. His volume, *Before the Mayflower,* has become required reading in many schools across the nation.

gus bertha—g.b. is a upsouth nigger (chgo; class of black realism) this nigger has got a lot to learn ( ) & poems are only a part as all abstract postures are but a prelude to. . . ./ it is a wild wish for my lifetime—but i too would like for once we'd meet & our voices would not be gruff.

Nora Blakely—is a student at the University of Illinois and the daughter of Gwendolyn Brooks.

Walter Bradford—Gemini. Poet/writer. Conducted a writers' workshop with a segment of the 63rd Street Black P. Stones. Went home to Africa in 1969. Published in *NOMMO, Black Expressions,* Broadside Press, *Journal of Black Poetry, Jump Bad, Black World.* A member of the OBAC Writers Workshop.

Patricia Brown—has been reading Gwendolyn Brooks since grade school. She is an instructor in African-American Literature and Communications Skills at Malcolm X Community College in Chicago.

f(rederick) j(ames) bryant jr.—was born and raised in Philadelphia, Pennsylvania. A 1967 graduate of Lincoln University (Pa.), he has had poems published in *Nickel Review, The Journal of Black Poetry, Negro Digest, Axiom,* and has been anthologized in *The New Black Poetry, Black Fire,* and *Extension.*

Margaret Taylor Goss Burroughs—artist, writer, teacher—is founder of Chicago DuSable Museum of African-American History. Her published works include *Jasper the Drummer Boy,* 1969; *Did You Feed My Cow,* 1969; *What Shall I Tell My Children,* 1968; and *Whip Me, Whop Me,* 1967.

john chenault—is a young poet living in Cincinnati, Ohio. *Blue Blackness* is the title of his first collection of poems. He conducts a Writers' Workshop.

Edward Christmas—"Christmas—Cultural Worker" is a Chicago photographer.

Carole Gregory Clemmons—born in Youngstown, Ohio, March 18, 1945, received her A.B. in English from Youngstown State University in 1968. Her poems have appeared in *Nine Black Poets* and *The New Black Poetry.* She is currently working for *Look Magazine* and is working on a manuscript.

Francois Clemmons—singer and writer, has been published in *Let America Sing,* a college anthology, and *Black World.* Presently a member of the Metropolitan (Opera) Studio, he has works scheduled for *Aim* and *A Galaxy of Black Writing.*

Cynthia M. Conley—"I am a Libra, am twenty-four, am Black. I live in Chicago, have two beautiful children and believe I am a Good Writer. Until I met Gwendolyn Brooks I wasn't nearly as sure of myself as I am now. She is my Mother-In-Writing and I Love Her."

james cunningham—"a 'Chicago' poet from St. Louis who fancies himself a blue shade of black critic & teacher born in 1936 as a Capricorn twin & post-Baldwinite whose true name is olumo. Whose contribution to black liberation is the pursuit of the rigorously examined life while touch-pushing the reader's sensibilities up against & hopefully over the 'wall' that poses as a sphinx-like limit somewhere on the edges of a break-thru."

Margaret Danner—of Chicago is in her third year as poet-in-residence at Virginia Union State University. She has been assistant editor of *Poetry Magazine,* poet-in-residence at Wayne State University, founder of Boone House for the Arts in Detroit, and of Nologonya's in Chicago. Published works include *Impressions of African Art Forms in Poetry,* 1962; *To Flower,* 1962; *Poem, Counterpoem* (with Dudley Randall), 1966; and *Iron Lace,* 1968.

R. M. Dennis—a Cincinnati writer, is a member of the writers' workshop headed by John Chenault.

Murry N. DePillars—Kuumba artist-in-residence, is a respected painter in the emerging school of black, revolutionary art. His works include the highly acclaimed "Black Christ" and "Aunt Jemima." A former art teacher, he is currently assistant director of the educational assistance program for minority students at the University of Illinois (Chicago Circle).

Alfred Diggs—a revolutionary black poet, currently is enduring democracy in Chicago and when not rapping black love, occupies space at the City College. He was born in Mishap (dats south they say) done time for whyte and is working on a collection of short stories. He has published one volume of poetry, *Naturally Black.*

Jeff Donaldson—is an award-winning Chicago artist and former lecturer in art at Northwestern University. He is the new head of the Art Department at Howard University.

Jon Eckels—born in Indianapolis, is the founder of *Uhuru,* a Black Community Newspaper. He has published one volume of poems, *Home Is Where the Soul Is.* He is currently teaching black poetry and literature in the Ethnic Studies Departments at Mills and Merritt Colleges.

Maxine Hall Elliston—aged twenty-four, was born and raised on the South Side of Chicago (39th Street). She is currently doing social work for a private agency. Her works have appeared in *Nommo* and *Negro Digest* and she has articles in *Film Comment.* "My proudest possession to date is an autographed copy of *The Wall* in which Gwendolyn says I am 'sassy and talented.'"

Sarah Webster Fabio—is an instructor at the University of California at Berkeley. Her poems and criticism have appeared regularly in *Negro Digest.* Her most recent volume is *A Mirror: A Soul, A Two-Part Volume of Poems.*

Hoyt W. Fuller—managing editor of *Black World* (formerly *Negro Digest*) was born in Atlanta, Georgia. A founder of the Organization of

Black American Culture, he is advisor to the OBAC Writers' Workshop.

Zack Gilbert—was a member of the Parkway Creative Writers' Forum during the late forties and early fifties. His works have appeared in *For Malcolm, Projection in Literature, Negro Digest,* and *The Liberator.* Presently an editorial consultant with the new black publishing company, Path Press, of Chicago, Mr. Gilbert is also working on scripts for an upcoming television series.

nikki giovanni—shares a birthday (June 7) with Gwendolyn Brooks. A 1967 graduate of Fisk University, she has published two volumes of poems, *Black Feeling, Black Talk,* 1968, and *Black Judgement,* 1969. Her book reviews have appeared regularly in *Negro Digest.* She lives in New York City with her son.

Joe Goncalves—born in Boston in 1937, has been a resident of San Francisco off and on since 1948. Presently he is editor of *The Journal of Black Poetry.*

Michael S. Harper—born March 18, 1938 in Brooklyn, New York, is married with two sons. "My debts are to the musicians: Trane, Miles, Bird, Bud, Lady Day, Pres, who taught me about style, *modal style,* in the face of terror and annihilation, and came through with resilience and sensibility beautified."

alicia l. johnson—was born February 27, 1944. She has published one volume of poems, *Realities vs. Spirits.* Other poems have appeared in *Black Arts, The Journal of Black Poetry, Negro Digest, Black Expressions, The New Black Poetry, Nine Black Poets,* and *Présence Africaine,* nos. 66 and 68.

Paulette Jones—age twenty-three, Chicago born, reared, and educated. A 1967 graduate of the University of Illinois, she is currently chairman of the writers' workshop at the university's Afro-American Cultural Center.

Raymond A. Joseph—a native of Puerto Rico, was reared in St. Thomas, Virgin Islands. Joseph is a senior at the University of Illinois, Champaign-Urbana, where he is majoring in creative writing.

Delores Kendrick—has had poems published in the U.S.A., Germany, Ireland, and Israel. Her narrative poem "Freddie" won the Deep South Writers' Award in 1966 and is now awaiting publication by Dasein Press in New York. Miss Kendrick is now on a sabbatical as a recipient of a fellowship in the Experienced Teacher Fellowship Program at Georgetown University.

John Oliver Killens—novelist, essayist, screen-writer and lecturer, presents a distinguished array of credits. His novels include *Youngblood, And Then He Heard the Thunder, 'Sippi,* and *Slaves.* His volume of essays, *Black Man's Burden* created a sensation when it first appeared in 1965. Articles and essays have appeared in numerous magazines and journals, including *Ebony, Negro Digest, New York Times Magazine, Holiday,* and *Redbook.* He is founder and former chairman of the Harlem Writers' Workshop and is vice president of the Black Academy of Arts and Letters. He is presently adjunct professor at Columbia University, where he leads a Black Culture seminar and a creative writing workshop. His latest novel, *Cotillion,* is due for publication in January, 1971.

Keorapetse Kgositsile—is from Johannesburg, South Africa and has been in exile since 1961. He has published two volumes of poetry, *Spirits Unchained* (Broadside Press, 1969) and *For Melba* (Third World Press, 1970). His poetry and essays have also appeared in *Guerilla, Journal of Black Poetry, Negro Digest, The New African, Pan African Journal, Black Arts, Black Fire* and *For Malcolm.* In 1969 he won the

Conrad Kent Rivers Memorial Award given by *Negro Digest.*

Helen H. King—a child of the ghetto, an *Ebony* assistant editor, author of a forthcoming black children's book, *Willy,* and the mother of two.

Etheridge Knight—"I was born on April 19, 1931, in Corinth, Mississippi, and I grew up in Paducah, Kentucky. I didn't finish the white man's high school—ran away from home instead; later, when I was seventeen years old, I joined the army disillusioned and hooked, and later went to prison disillusioned and hooked. Came out of prison a year ago with no illusions and not hooked. Am now in love. With me, my wife and children, and my people."

Pinkie Gordon Lane—the first black woman to receive a Ph.D. from Louisiana State University (1967), is a professor of English at Southern University. Her poems have appeared in *Phylon, The National Poetry Anthology, The Personalist,* and *South and West,* a literary quarterly. Poems appear in *Contemporary American Negro Poets.*

don l. lee—poet, essayist, critic, is currently a lecturer in Afro-American Literature at the University of Illinois in Chicago. He formerly held the same position at Cornell University. He has published four volumes of poetry, *Think Black; Black Pride; Don't Cry, Scream;* and *We Walk the Way of the New World,* all published by Broadside Press. He is currently completing a book of criticism on black poets of the sixties. His work, including book reviews, has appeared in *Negro Digest, The Journal of Black History, Evergreen Review, The New York Times, Muhammed Speaks, Freedomways, Liberator, Free Lance, Nommo, The Chicago Daily Defender, Ebony,* and others.

David Llorens—has worked as a SNCC activist in Mississippi, a newspaper reporter in his native Chicago, assistant editor of *Negro Digest* and associate editor of *Ebony*. An outstanding essayist, he considers himself primarily a prose writer although one critic has described his poems as "worth waiting for." He currently teaches black literature at the University of Washington (Seattle), where he is an assistant professor of English, and is at work on a book about LeRoi Jones for Frederick Praeger.

Jon Lockard—is an artist and a graduate student at the University of Michigan (Ann Arbor).

James C. Morris—writer and teacher, has published two volumes, *Cleopatra and Other Poems*, 1955, and *From a Tin-Mouth God to His Grass-Eared Subjects*, 1967. He has co-authored a reading series for the New York City Board of Education, Call Them Heroes. He is a member of the Three Penny Poets in New York City.

Rukudzo Murapa—is a writer from Zimbabwe (Rhodesia) whose work has appeared in *Negro Digest* and other black publications. He is currently assistant professor at the African Studies and Research Center—Black Studies Program of Cornell University.

Larry Neal—was born in 1937 in Atlanta, Georgia, and was reared in Philadelphia. His work has been published in *Ebony*, *Freedomways*, *Negro Digest*, *Soulbook*, and *The Journal of Black Poetry*. He co-edited, with Leroi Jones, the anthology, *Black Fire*.

Tejumola Ologboni—born Rockie Taylor, is a Milwaukee poet whose first published volume, *Drum Song*, contains an introduction by Gwendolyn Brooks.

Eugene Perkins—author of two volumes of poetry—*An Apology to my African Brother* and *Black is Beautiful*, is founder/editor of Free Black Press and program director of Better Boys Foundation on Chicago's West Side.

Sterling D. Plumpp—born in Clinton, Miss., in 1940, he grew up on a cotton farm under his grandfather's supervision. He began to write fiction in the army, later switched to poetry. He has published two volumes of poetry, *Portable Soul* and *Half-Black, Half-Blacker.*

Dudley Randall—poet-in-residence at the University of Detroit, is founder of Broadside Press. His published works include *Poem, Counterpoem* (with Margaret Danner), 1966; *For Malcolm* (co-edited with Margaret Burroughs), 1967; and *Black Poetry* (editor), 1969.

barbara a reynolds—a former staff writer for *Ebony*, is currently a reporter for *Chicago Today*, one of Chicago's four major daily newspapers. Her work has appeared in *Negro Digest*.

Carolyn M. Rodgers—Chicago-born poetess who recently published her third volume, *Songs of a Black Bird*. Her earlier books were *Paper Soul* and *Two Love Raps*. Carolyn is a member of OBAC in Chicago, and won the first annual Conrad Kent Rivers writing award in 1968.

sonia sanchez (knight)—"mwimbji—blk/woman/mother/teacher/poet/ playwright barely surviving in wh/america. like that record be sayen: it ain't easy."

sharon scott—although one of the youngest members (in age) of the Gwendolyn Brooks Writers' Workshop, is a senior member of that group. A freshman at Fisk University, she is at work on her first volume, a joint effort with two other Fisk students.

Robert Sengstacke—Chicago photographer, is currently photographer-in-residence at Fisk University. His works have appeared in numerous exhibits in the Chicago area as well as in such publications as *Negro Digest*. His first book is in preparation for publication.

Linwood Smith—received his B.A. from Gallaudet College in Washington, D.C. in 1965. A former collegiate track star, he now lives and teaches the deaf in Raleigh, North Carolina. He has studied under Arthur P. Davis *(Negro Caravan)*, and Dr. Lewis Henderson *(Many Shades of Black)*. His writings have appeared in *Encore, Simbolica, Negro Voices, Cyclo-Flame,* and *Clover Poets Anthology.*

A. B. Spellman—poet and jazz authority, is currently at work on a biography of Billie Holiday. Previously published work includes *Four Lives in the Be-Bop Business* and *The Beautiful Day and Others.*

prentiss taylor jr.—"Am especially inspired by Emory West, Bob Kaufman, Leon Damas, and Gylan Kain. Am working with the OUT-REACH program for Roxbury-Dorchester alcoholics. Am, as Gwen would probably say, one of the 'sweaty and unpretty' niggahs at Harvard. Am hoping to compile an anthology of poems by and for black college students, soon. Am Chicago flavored in my yeah."

Joe Todd—a Cincinnati writer, is a member of the writer's workshop headed by john chenault.

Margaret Walker—professor of English at Jackson (Miss.) State College, achieved national prominence with her volume of poetry, *For My People,* 1942, for which she was awarded the Yale University Younger Poets Prize. She gained further distinction with the novel *Jubilee,* 1967, the winner of the Houghton, Mifflin Literary Fellowship Award.

Bruce Walton—born in slavery August 12, 1942, in Johnstown, Pennsylvania, is chairman of the United Black Association at the University of Cincinnati, where he is a graduate student in community planning.

w. d. wandick—a student at Northeastern Illinois State College, is a former student of Gwendolyn Brooks.

Francis Ward—former associate editor of *Jet* and assistant editor of *Ebony,* joined the staff of the *Chicago Sun-Times* in 1968. He is currently midwest correspondent in the Chicago bureau of the *Los Angeles Times.*

Val Gray Ward—"The Voice of the Black Writer" has become one of the most successful and widely imitated actresses in the country through her sensitive interpretations of the writing of black authors, past and present. Mrs. Francis Ward in private life, she is former director of the Afro-American Cultural Center at the University of Illinois, Champaign–Urbana.

Sigemonde Kharlos Wimberli—is editor of the Community Newspaper, *The Black Truth,* on Chicago's West Side. He is also a member of the OBAC Writers' Workshop. *Ghetto Scenes* is the title of his first book of poems.